Through Tragedy and Triumph

A Life Well Traveled

Hagir Elsheikh

with
Tom Peashey

ISBN: 9781091595958

Cover design: Deb Sutton

Contents

Remembrance

You are about to read about my life, a life full of experience, a life sometimes full of tragedy. But, always a life full of challenges and a determination to make a better life – not only for myself and my family – but for all my life touches.

This dedication to serve the needs of all around me was instilled in me by my father – Seed Ahmed Elsheikh – our Elhakeem. A medical man, he spent his life doing what he could with so little – never enough medicine and inadequate facilities for those in need, but he was more than a caregiver. When he saw wrong – he tried to right it. When he saw starvation – he looked for food for others. When he saw oppression and brutal domination – he took to the streets and fought peacefully for change, for freedom, for peace. With many sons, he still taught his daughters that they were equal, that with education and determination, his daughters could accomplish as much as any of his sons. He instilled all this into his large brood of children, especially his thirteenth and final child.

All I have learned, all I have strived for, my compassion for anyone who enters into my realm of reality. All this I owe to my father. I remember him every day. I remember him when I look into my children's eyes. When I see suffering and hurt, I ask, "What would Father want me to do?" I have dedicated my life to the memory of my father, my Elhakeem.

Dedication

To my two beautiful girls, my wings who kept me flying, *Malaz* and *Remaz*. Thank you for being my right hand and my support through it all. For the sleepless nights and early mornings and for understanding my struggle, for the long hours I spent away from you so I can give you a better future. You are growing up to be everything a mother can ask for and more.

Preface

It was difficult, at first, to reach back into the recesses of my mind to recount the details of my past, but once I began, the memories flooded back in a torrent, as crystal clear as water. Waves of information flowed through me, each detail fighting for precedence, demanding to jump to the front of the line: people, places, things, experiences, heartache, challenges and triumphs – so much to be shared. Once the dam was opened, the deluge of information washed over me and left me with but one regret: that I didn't begin the memoir writing process sooner.

Now that I'm finally getting the words down on paper, my hope is that my trials and triumphs will be an inspiration to others and will empower readers across the globe as many have been an inspiration to me during my journey. My intent is for everyone to read my story and to view it as a story of hope.

As a young girl in Sudan, I faced many obstacles, and unfortunately, those obstacles continued throughout my adulthood. Women continue to struggle every day and not just in Sudan but even here in the United States. Women face an uphill battle, from sexism and violence to inequality. In some areas, they are forced to deal with a culture that promotes primitive practices that endanger them, not just physically, but emotionally as well.

As a woman myself, I struggled and had to fight for my rights from the day I was born. I'm sure I will continue fighting until the day I die. At an early age and long before I knew my road would be filled with obstacles, I was at the receiving end to one of the most horrible experiences any child can face. That was the practice of Female Genital Mutilation or FGM.

One of the most inhumane practices became one of the topics that I currently speak about in an effort to educate others. I was a victim, despite my father's efforts to prevent it from happening. My

3

grandmother worked around my father to insure that this inhumane act was performed on both me and my sister. Despite his being dead set against this, she feared the social stigma of not complying with the accepted mores more than she feared her son. I still remember it very well, although I was very young at the time. Not only did we suffer the mental and physical effects of this insidious practice, but the sense of mistrust became positively profound.

FGM and many other issues are taboo to discuss in areas like Sudan. To utter them aloud is unacceptable. To speak of them in public is absolutely unheard of. The only reason I was able to share my story is because I was raised by a very unique and open-minded family who taught me from the beginning that I was no different from my brothers... that as a woman, I could do everything that my brothers could do. I learned that sometimes I can even do things better!

Women raised in what others deem a "third-world country" face many challenges by virtue of being born, from unfair treatment by men to being viewed by society as a burden. Low self-esteem becomes part of one's persona when society treats you as useless and unwanted. This feeling can haunt and hurt you unless you take measures to try to change it. For many, it's not easy. A few lucky ones who were raised by liberal families have the advantage of being treated with some freedom and fairness, but it rarely exists beyond that family unit. Females develop relationships in their neighborhood and their schools where the message is instilled in them that they are less of a person simply by virtue of being female. There are so many unspoken roles and issues that women face and are forced to deal with on a daily basis; I will try to explore some of them here as much as possible.

Women have the ability to build communities, run countries, work in various occupations, hold an array of titles and raise

4

generations of children. They are capable of fighting for equality and fairness while standing against discrimination and violence. Women, please celebrate who you are and believe that you can make a difference every day. You are limitless; don't allow anyone to convince you otherwise and understand that the most vital information to keep in mind is that independence is the answer to many problems. If I wasn't independent from the onset, my story may have been different. This is why I encourage others to find a way to attend school and earn a degree, get a job and learn how to take care of yourself.

I struggled a lot; as a human rights and a woman rights activist, I was tortured, lashed, whipped, detained and at some point hanged from my wrists in a tree to be beaten more. During college, the torture continued until I fled the country and immigrated to the US. Then as an adult, I was in a physically and mentally abusive relationship. I was choked, hit with objects even while I was pregnant, dragged bleeding and threatened so many times. I dealt with a lot; anything that could go wrong with any one person happened to me at some point in my life. I didn't let this define me, control my destiny, or dictate how I will live the rest of my life.

So far in my life, I've been an engineer, a nurse, a teacher, a business owner, a CEO of a non-profit who help raise awareness about domestic violence especially and violence in general. I've been a host to a TV talk show and a co-host to a radio show. I've been on both sides: a victim of domestic violence and an advocate for survivors. I needed help at some point in my life, and I helped others at some point. I've been a spokesperson to fight for human rights and a motivational speaker to inspire others. I've been a volunteer who felt that I was alive to give back, and most importantly, I've been a single mother to the most beautiful human beings I have ever seen. I will do anything in my power to ensure this world is a better place for my kids and my community.

I will explain many of the inhuman things that happened from the day I was born until today, but I also choose not to give them any more control over my life. I will share the good things and how I manage to turn the ugly into beautiful and the sad times into lessons for me and others. I believe, in order for you to change your life, you must change your surroundings by taking small steps. You have the power within you and you may surprise yourself, but you have to take that first step. Many people think it is impossible to succeed when all of the signs point to your failure. I look at it as a challenge to succeed against the odds and have that sense of accomplishment and personal growth during those hard times.

Chapter 1

THE UNSUNG STORY OF SUDAN
Climbing on the Clouds

The precious and precocious four-year-old had been walking for some time. It might have been twenty minutes or perhaps two hours. To one so young, time loses relevance. Her eyes reflected the desert sun and gave her a radiance that foretold the Nubian beauty she would become.

I smiled and continued my journey. "I'm coming. I'm coming!" I exclaimed, loud enough that anyone in earshot would wonder who I was talking to. Who indeed? But, I proceeded on through the desert sand – my quest seemingly within reach.

I was a curious child with a rich imagination. This vivid memory started when I was looking at the sky from our front door. There was limitless sand with no houses in front of me. For as far as my vision could see, there was nothing ahead but a clear blue sky that seemed never-ending. I thought there was an area ahead where the sky would meet the earth. So, I went on an adventure to find it. My plan was that once I found where the sky and earth collided, I would climb onto the clouds. I would use those clouds as my own personal passageway. A passageway to where? Perhaps one to wherever a child's dreams might bring me. My wild imagination had no limits. Of course, I didn't think through how I would ever exit the clouds.

I started walking, looking for that area where the sky and earth meet. I don't remember how far I walked or for how long. Fortunately, some farmers from a nearby village were passing by on their donkeys and saw me wandering in the desert and stopped me.

"Little one… where are you going?" one of the farmers asked. I just pointed off into the distance, smiled and said nothing.

"But, you have no water. The desert is not a kind master, child. Where do you come from?" I just pointed back towards the city.

Finally, I spoke, "I'm going there where the blue sky meets the sand. When I get there, I'll climb onto the clouds. I'll ride them across the sky." I smiled sweetly as if this was the most normal quest for any child to achieve. I folded my arms, extended my chest with pride and gave them a confident look – one way beyond my years. The farmers gave a knowing laugh and just shook their heads.

"Who is your father, child?" one asked as he reached out his large, calloused hand and took mine firmly but gently.

Soon enough, they knew I was Elhakeem's daughter. The villagers adored my father whom they deemed "Elhakeem" which translates to "Doctor" in Arabic and also means "the wise man". In reality, he was the equivalent of a Physician's Assistant, a well educated medical person who was critical to the survival of the people of this outlying area.

They put me on one of their donkeys and took me back home laughing, again, at my attempt.

The farmer lifted me off the small beast of burden and brought me to my front door. My father opened the door and asked, "Hagir, what have you done?"

The farmer's smile gave some relief to Father's concern. "Elhakeem, perhaps she can explain it better, but I found her wandering several kilometers out in the desert west of the city. You have quite the child here. It seems she was traveling to where the sky meets the sand. She apparently planned to go *Climbing On The Clouds*."

My father laughed very hard and thanked the farmer, told him he owed him a favor that would be repaid and sent him on his way. He looked at me, smiled – shaking his head slightly at the brilliance and imagination of his thirteenth and youngest child – and sat me down to explain my error and the danger I put myself in. That was his way. He never laid hands on us but always used our mistakes as a teaching moment to reason with us and tell us what we did wrong. He would provide a solution or another route we could've taken.

When he finished, I just looked up at him with the angelic expression only one so young could master, disappointed but still smiling and asked so innocently, "So, I can't climb on the clouds? Why?"

Elhakeem just smiled, shook his head and reached for the tiny, cherubic hand that belonged to his youngest child. "Come little one; perhaps mother can explain it better."

Chapter 2

Loving Parents
Elhakeem–Seed Ahmed & Buthina

Father was still perhaps a little bewildered by the creative mind of his youngest and the way I perceived the world... even at that young age. Everything seemed possible to me. I already saw life as just one challenge after another for me to overcome – and I would.

After his best attempt to explain the sky and even a bit about the world being round, Father added, "Hagir, when you are older, you will be able to achieve anything you put your mind to. You may never be able to walk on the clouds, but you most certainly will fly over them as you take on the world and make it a better place. Come little one; let's go tell your mother about the clouds." His life lesson ended in a firm hug from the man I loved more than any other.

His way of raising us was because of his beliefs in making a difference and changing his community's ways of dealing with issues. His political views and beliefs landed him in a leadership role in his community. He was a fighter and he paid a very high price for his involvement. He was often detained and kept away from his kids. One of those times, he was detained during my mom's pregnancy with my sister, Nagla, and he wasn't released until the day she was born. My mom was at the receiving end of this, as well. She had to take care of a newborn, all the other kids, the household and all their needs on her own. My siblings weren't old enough to help much at that time.

My dad traveled a lot due to his job, and he helped anywhere needed. That's why almost all my siblings were born in different cities. I was the youngest of thirteen. I believe I was an "oops" child. My parents decided to stop after my sister Nagla was born, and they did for five years, then I came as a surprise. Maybe I wasn't a planned pregnancy, but they never made me feel as such. My parents' first born died at the age of one; at that time, my mom was pregnant with my oldest brother Rashid. Having a large family wasn't an unusual thing in Sudan. Most people don't use or believe in birth control.

As you can see, my father was a wise and kind man. His kindness seemed to know no bounds, and he availed himself to anyone who needed him no matter the time of day. I remember him leaving in the middle of the night or the early morning to help the sick, administer an injection, or simply check a patient to ensure they were alright.

Despite his demanding schedule, he was always upbeat and wearing a smile. If he was tired or upset, he certainly didn't show it. The people of Tandalti adored him, as did his family. His dedication to others and focus on doing the right thing inspired me and my siblings to imitate him. To witness the love and respect that he received from those families was enough to help us understand how special he was to everyone.

Father brought me into the kitchen area. "Buthina, your youngest is up to it again. Her curiosity and imagination continue to amaze." He sat me at the kitchen table and Mother leaned in and kissed my forehead.

She sat next to me, smiled lovingly and asked, "Child, what have you done now?"

Father explained my quest and there were more than a few smiles and even contagious laughter which I didn't understand other than to realize that I wasn't really in trouble.

As for my mother, my memories of her are as bright as the sky on a sunny day. Buthina Ibrahim (Muslim women do not take the last name of their husbands) was a stay-at-home mom, like most of the mothers in Sudan at that time. It was she who tended to household affairs like cooking, cleaning, raising the kids, and grocery shopping.

I recall that she was the first one up and the last one to go to sleep. For a long time, I was unaware that she slept at all. In my young mind, she was comparable to a superhero, like Wonder Woman. She never complained about being tired and never asked for anything for herself. To this day, I envision her wearing the same dress, sweeping the floor or toiling by the fire in the small kitchen area as sweat dripped from her forehead.

Kindly, sweet and calm are words that come to mind when describing her. That's not to say that she never became upset. When she did, you could tell by the expression on her face which more closely registered disappointment over anger. Rather than lash out, she would become very quiet and drift away. During those times, she continued to take care of the household by completing chores and ensuring that everything was in order. She would nurse the sick at home and carry on without complaint.

I remember waking up in the middle of the night sometimes to see her bustling about, covering us quietly with blankets while we slept or waking one of my siblings to administer water or medicine. Every now and again we would overhear her singing in her indescribably beautiful voice. If she sensed someone was listening, she'd fall silent while continuing about her business so as not to call attention to herself.

She'd listen to the radio quite a bit while working. Sometimes, she'd listen to music and other times, the news... which rarely reported anything good. She would become so worried when she would learn about something bad happening anywhere, especially if it were in a country where her children or other family members resided. She fretted about our fate and was especially anxious for me with my political involvement resulting in numerous detentions. She cried often back then. When I would arrive home with a bruise after a rally, she would make it her job to take care of me. One of the most difficult things to witness was the pain in her eyes as she tried to heal me. At that time, I wished I could have taken that pain away. I wished I could have reassured her that all would be well, but I had no guarantee. I will forever be grateful for her existence in my life and for everything she's done.

My mother was the thread that held everything together. She was the foundation of my success, and her sacrifices are the reason that I am where I am today. Even when I was in college, I always found comfort lying next to her, feeling her fingers brushing my hair or giving me kisses on my cheek and forehead. Her unique scent, a mixture of oil, perfume, and her natural smell was the scent that could make me feel safe. It is so distinct, and I've locked it away in my memories, hoping that I would never forget it. When I began to miss her, I would think of her scent and reminisce about those moments with her even for a split second. She didn't talk much but her body language and her facial expressions said a lot. Up to this point in my life, I have always referred to her values and the ethics that she taught us. She is a big believer that actions speak louder than words.

She is a very traditional woman, just like so many at her age who grew up in an environment that treats women as a second-class citizen and did believe that the woman's place was at home. Her father took her out of school just a few weeks after she started. She still gets choked up whenever she tells that story. Mom told me that despite her father's wishes to keep her home, those few weeks in school were some of her favorite memories. She wanted to learn. Her desire reached beyond housekeeping and society's typical "woman's responsibilities". At an early age, she learned how to cook, sew, and take care of the house with her other sisters. Of course, her brothers had a chance to attend school. I can't imagine how she must have felt knowing that there was an opportunity for

13

her to become anything, and because she was a female, that opportunity was taken from her. Life could've been so different if she had been given the chance to attend school.

She told me that her relationship with my father, her husband, started on their wedding day. It was an arranged marriage... like most of the marriages back then in Sudan. She was very young and basically moved from her father's house to her husband's house. She was expected to take care of the house and later, the kids. I don't believe she was ever given the chance to even know or think about what she wanted. How could she? She grew up in a time where thinking and dreaming was a crime for women.

This definitely affected her life, but it didn't change how she treated us or others. She wore a smile on her face all the time. Regardless of how much my father was involved and helpful to her, she was still the main one to complete the household chores. My father was expected to only work outside, but he broke that stigma by helping out where he could.

Thinking of my mother and the vital role she played in my life makes me realize how lucky I am to have a mother. I have met many people who were raised without a mother and others whose mother had little involvement in their lives. I know what effect that has had on their future.

I can't imagine my life if it weren't for her and my father modeling the behavior that they expected of us. Because of their influence and others', I try to be a good role model for my kids and use my parents' method with my girls. Sometimes, I find myself just like any other mother who will use her power to win any fight or argument with their kids. I take this direction sometimes and I yell at them when they make a mistake, but then, I remember how mom and dad's method worked better and I redirect myself. Their method helped me develop a close relationship with my girls. They know that I am still growing and learning alongside them.

My mother and father were loved and thought of very highly by everyone in the village. The way they treated and cared for the villagers left a lasting impact not only on the people whom they helped but also on me. It was rare to see them sad or stressed. Not because they didn't have issues in their lives, but because they always tried so hard to shield and protect us.

I was most fortunate to have been born into a family where the parents' traditional upbringing did not determine how they raised their own children. They rejected the Islamic Conservatism that was forced on Sudan and ensured that their children – all their children – were educated and prepared to succeed in a most difficult world.

Chapter 3

Like Father – Like Daughter

As the ambulance rounded the bend, Seed Ahmed could see the compound ahead. The driver looked at him with great concern.

"Elhakeem, what if the soldiers have not left yet? Are you sure you wish to proceed? Is it safe?"

The doctor just laughed cautiously. "Are we safe anywhere? That young farmer said there were hundreds here who needed our help. We must go on."

Here in the White Nile State, conflicts between the poor farmers – loosely organized into Labor Unions – and the Government in Khartoum were all too common and often, too deadly. It was usually well-equipped soldiers against underpaid, starving workers who merely wanted what was promised to them – with little more than farm equipment and machetes. Primarily, the farmers were mostly indigenous tribesmen while the army consisted mainly of Arab Conservative Muslims. Internationally, it was a well-known secret that mass graves dotted the countryside.

The ambulance pulled into the compound, and they began searching the buildings.

"Elhakeem, in here." Seed Ahmed found his driver staring at a door nailed shut by a large, wooden cross. Quickly, they found some discarded tools and after some work, were able to free the door.

They froze as they stared into the room. How could so many be squashed into such a small space? Nothing moved! Not a sound other than the choking breaths of anger and grief from the rescuers. The bodies were piled on top of each other. Near the top of the pile, they could see some young boys – just children. Looking up, they saw the smallest air hole – the only source of breathable air in the desert heat. It was obvious that the older men in one final selfless act

16

had raised the children to be closest to the air and possible survival. It was fruitless. All were gone in a horrid execution that made the Nazi gas chambers seem humane – three hundred in total. The Anbar Godah massacre was now a tragic part of the history of the world – an example of what can happen when human morality decays to a point of infamy.

My father was born somewhere between 1929 and 1930 in the small city of Al Kamlin some fifty-three miles from the capital city of Khartoum. At a young age, he found work as a doorman at the local hospital. Over time, he was able to enter the school of nursing – working and studying simultaneously. After graduating as a registered nurse, he continued his studies and became a surgical technician; this was about equivalent to what we now call a PA, Physician's Assistant. He always continued studying and climbing the ladder from bottom to top. He never felt any job was beneath him and was the true meaning of a self-made man – an example for all to follow. Finally, one of the leading doctors in the surgery (operating hospital) who had trained him, retired, and Seed Ahmed was promoted to replace him. He reverently became "Elhakeem".

My father constantly tried to educate everyone around him – he believed education was the key to everything. The fragile, young government in Khartoum was beginning to become more and more fearful of these political activists – particularly in the rapidly forming labor unions. They often targeted the political activists and began to exile them to other areas as a form of punishment. Dad was sent to the impoverished Northern Darfur region in the west where, instead of seeing it as punishment, he saw it as a new opportunity and challenge. He soon began to educate the people in this new territory as to what their rights were and even started a union. He was moved often throughout the Darfur region. His political activism started soon after World War II, and by 1949, he was fighting for the independence of Sudan from the British Empire. Over the years, he was one of the founders of the National Nurses Association and was a member of the General Federation of Workers Trade Union as well as the Workers Affairs Association among other groups who dealt with the welfare of all laborers. Soon, he became one of the union leaders and a little later was Secretary of the Union in the city of Kosti (Kusti), capital of the White Nile State. It was his associations with these unions in that State south of Khartoum that saw him become one of the contributors to the White Nile Farmers Union. This is why when one of the farmers, though severely wounded, escaped and lived to tell the story, he immediately went to Seed Ahmed's hospital where he knew he would find a friend.

The farm laborers had been cheated of their meager wages; all their hard work had gone for naught. With the encouragement of men like the good Elhakeem, they stood their ground and were prepared to fight. The farmers made their demands for what was due to them, and a corrupt, greedy government met them with bullets, killing many and rounding up as prisoners some 300 who had escaped the quick death of a bullet. They were herded into a small room with no windows and only one small air vent in the ceiling. Mostly men and some young boys, with no food, water and such a confined space, they soon succumbed to the desert heat and lack of oxygen. Reports have as many as seventeen hundred dying that day, but these three hundred were the last to pass and certainly, they would have been much better off to have joined their brothers who were spared the agony and desperation of the slow execution by suffocation and dehydration.

"Elhakeem, what shall we do?" one of the workers asked.

Through his tears, he answered, "We must bury our friends and bring word of their sacrifice for justice and freedom to the rest of the world. Come, we have much work to do."

Father and his few friends buried their fellow workers ten to a grave until all three hundred had been laid to rest. He would not have even been there if it weren't for that one worker who escaped and even though severely wounded, made it to my father's hospital and asked for him by name. Seed Ahmed was immediately sent for and raced to the hospital where he heard the story of both bravery and savage brutality. He immediately arranged with one of the hospital administrators that he be allowed to take an ambulance and a few men and go to the site to search for and assist any survivors. For the rescuers, there was nothing more for them to do except bury their dead neighbors and friends.

Near the bottom of the pile, anguish overcame Elhakeem as he found the body his friend, the President of the Farmer's Union. He was a witness that day to a horrible crime against humanity, one that saw the perpetrators go unpunished. Unfortunately, that day was more the beginning – not the end – of the fighting. This massacre near Godah, Sudan was only one of many, and it occurred shortly after independence was granted in 1956. It was just one mass grave site among many. The struggle still continues over sixty years later to correct the atrocities that began after independence. Every time Father related the events of that day, he did so with tears rolling down his cheeks and the stain of brutal, total anguish on his face – the memories of the Anbar Godah Massacre still fresh in his mind.

Father continued fighting and raising awareness while saving lives at his hospital until the day he died. He instilled in all of his children that fighting for the dignity of man and the rights of all was essential to leading a good life and that education was the path to being able to accomplish that goal. I would like to think that with every difficult road I travelled, I made my father proud that he had instilled in his thirteenth and youngest child the spirit of a fighter for the rights and freedoms of all human beings – no matter the race, religion or gender.

Chapter 4

Tandalti, Sudan

As I reflect back on the small city in Sudan where I was born, details of my life there are as clear as if they occurred just yesterday. It's ironic that sometimes I can't remember what happened two weeks ago, but I can remember things from my childhood. I can recount the smallest feeling of the sands on my bare feet to the smell of the rain on the sandy walls of our house. My father, always the medical professional, spent his days (and often nights) helping the underprivileged. He was so passionate about his work. He often traveled with our family tagging along with him from one place to another. As a child, I didn't understand that his frequent moves were an attempt by the government to negate his rabble-rousing activities while still keeping his valuable medical services available. Tandalti is a small town of around 27,000 in White Nile State, Central Sudan on the border between White Nile State and Northern Kordofan State. I'm told that on January 9th, 1977, I was welcomed into this world and with my parent's passion for life, equality and fairness for all – they began to mold the person I have become today.

I remember Tandalti and the villages near it vividly: from the weathered faces of the farmers to the animals that accompanied them. They arrived at our house every morning to fill up water vessels of all shapes and sizes. Our house served as a gathering place of sorts, where the villagers congregated to collect the water they needed for the day. The workers who lived near the hospital were the only individuals who had easy access to water and electricity – others were forced to walk long distances. My father, sympathetic to their plight, invited them to his home to gather what they needed for the day every day. I recall with fondness the long, snaking line to the faucet, because as a child, this translated into amusement for me through the companionship provided by the little girls and boys who arrived with their families. They taught me how to ride donkeys and horses, and they were an endless source of fun. Of course, I felt lonely and sad when they left, but it was something that I looked forward to the next morning. There were not a lot of things for children to do in our village, especially after sundown. Occasionally, I played with some kids who lived near us. Mostly simple games, such as hide and seek and some made up games. I don't remember those times clearly except for one activity, playing in the sand.

Playing in the sand was one of the activities that I enjoyed. Tandalti was known for the endless sand. I remember thinking about this village as a sand factory. I would sit for many hours wondering how it was possible to have a rain shower and soon after the rain had stopped you could leave your house and walk on it without getting dirty. How is it possible not to have mud puddles? I used to walk and try to trace my steps. To my surprise, any time I lifted my foot off the sand it filled right back with no evidence of my impression. In my young mind, I thought there was a magical aspect to it.

While as the medical man's family we had more than most, I do have some early memories that point out the poverty of the area. If we were considered "well off", then you can imagine the plight of the majority of the people.

I remember well that we didn't have an actual kitchen table. It was more like a piece of old metal surrounded by plastic covered chairs. This small, round metal table acted more as a kind of end table. The beds in the room would become multi-functional as we would sit on the beds during the day and huddle around that small metal table – talking, eating or drinking coffee or tea. The chairs and beds were circled at meals and became our dining room. There was also a large metal tray which was used to carry food and breads. Normally, the whole family ate together from the same plate using the bread for dipping in a main dish plate. Sometimes, there was a salad plate to share and they often had homemade bread like material called Gurasah, along with Kisrah which is a thin form of bread that tastes different but is very popular in Sudan and a staple of their main traditional meal. Both of these were cheaper than buying bread. At night, the beds reverted to their original use – sleeping.

I smile as one of my early memories was of the simple task of brushing my teeth. Toothpaste was a luxury rather than a necessity. When we did have it, we used every last drop – and I do mean LAST DROP. We rolled the tube all the way from the end, squeezing every small bit, and then, we cut the end of the tube off and rubbed our toothbrush inside to get the final remnants. Only when the tube was sparkling clean of every bit of toothpaste, would we buy more – IF there was money to do so. If there was no money, we made do with what was left of the bath soap – not very tasty… but effective.

Then, we would move on to the dish soap which was a hard abrasive, not a liquid. You would feel the burning and the sting on your gums, but you had to use it regardless to brush your teeth. That memory stays in your mouth for quite a while, lingering there and messing up everything else you eat and introduce to your taste buds – not something I'll easily forget. Such was the reality of Tandalti. From its unpaved streets to the endless desert sands, life as I remember it in one of the poorest regions of the world was never easy for anyone.

Chapter 5

Amal – Too Young to Grieve

My parents showed strength and happiness regardless of their circumstances except for a life-altering event, and unfortunately, we encountered one; it was the loss of one of my sisters.

My father seemed so sad. He simply looked at me, gave me a hug and said, "Hagir, you will not go into the back room." I knew something was very wrong, but was too young to ask the right questions.

My oldest brother, Rashid – who was already well into his twenty's – took me by the hand and said, "Come little one. Let's sit over here and let me try and explain."

I remember clearly the passing of my sister Amal. Amal is an Arabic name meaning Hope. Amal was in high school, and I was just shy of my seventh birthday. At that time, I was too young to understand why everyone around me was so sad, why they were crying. I never saw my mom and dad as sad as they were that day. I remember hearing people talking about Amal and how sweet she was. We had many visitors that day. I remember her skinny body under a white sheet lying in the middle of an empty room. Traditional pre-burial scents filled the room. In Sudan, there were no funeral homes, and families had to prepare the deceased's body themselves. Typically, an experienced elderly person performs the ritualistic preparation: they prepare an empty area in the house to bathe the body, using different kinds of natural elements to preserve the body. Normally, they have to bury the deceased the same day. These pre-burial rituals in Sudan are deeply rooted in the culture from both religious belief and tradition. In our case, like many other cases in Sudan, people become so occupied with the death and the ritual that they don't think about their children.

I don't think they ever thought of the psychological effect death can have on a young mind. I didn't understand what was going on, but I remember crying as a result of seeing my family cry. That day I don't believe I ever saw my mother or father cry. I never questioned that until later on when my brother Rashid mentioned that he had the same concern until few days after her passing. That day, my dad was calling the kids to get him something from the other side of the house and he called her name; he called for Amal. At that moment, I believe it hit him, and he realized she was gone. They said he was crying so hard – the sobbing grief only a parent can understand.

But, I don't recall any of that. I don't remember either mom or dad talking about her or even mentioning her name. This day changed the whole family and the family dynamics, and it went unmentioned for a long time. It felt to me as if they were trying to erase her memory or to avoid living the bad memory of her passing over and over again just by mentioning her name. Amal was beautiful and full of life. It was hard for me to understand how she was there one day and gone the next. This, I believe, was my first encounter with death and loss.

Later on, I learned she died because of complications possibly caused by a misdiagnosis. They said she had a very bad case of Malaria which was all too common. My uncle who had been taught by my father to assist in medical matters was giving her a strong injection to treat malaria. Some said the side effect of the medication affected her kidney and caused kidney failure. Others thought she had something else and that the wrong treatment caused her death. This is one of the issues that Sudanese people often encounter. Misdiagnosed and treatment without proper knowledge of the disorder or the disease is common.

Black Fever was one of the diagnoses that I learned later had similar symptoms and very likely was what she had contracted.

Black Fever is a chronic and potentially fatal parasitic disease that affects the liver, spleen, bone marrow and lymph nodes. It's transmitted by sand fly bites. Kala-Azar is a slow progressing, indigenous disease caused by protozoan parasites and could have been contracted years earlier. This would explain much about Amal – especially why she was so thin. She was buried in Tandalti which is why my feelings toward the place of my birth are quite mixed. I feel a special connection to it because that's where she is, but I have a sort of resentment knowing that it was being in that place that took my sister. In reflection, it's highly likely that she was infected much earlier – even before I was born – when the family was moving around the Darfur region. But, that doesn't dull the pain I felt at such a young age losing my beautiful older, teenaged sister. Amal passed in September of 1983.

I sometimes feel that my brain is a huge building with many rooms, closets and hidden spaces. When it comes to memories of Amal and the other siblings who passed which we'll discuss later, I must search this house in my brain and climb up to leave those very dark, hidden spots and come out into the light to remember my beautiful, teenaged sister who was so close and one of my caretakers. I got the feeling from the adults that losing children before they could even begin to think about adult life and how they could contribute to the world was such a normal occurrence in Sudan that they were really not able to rationalize why. Though my parents weren't particularly religious, even they seemed to simply accept the loss of a child as simply God's will. When it came to death, they gave it religious reasons.

Chapter 6

FGM – Female Genital Mutilation

My second feeling of loss spoiling my childhood memories in Tandalti was my experience with Female Circumcision or what is more accurately called Female Genital Mutilation (FGM).

Mother opened the door and there were both of my grandmothers and two of my aunts – both Mother's sisters. They came in and soon others joined. There was food and celebration – much singing and moments of excitement that seemed to revolve around me and my older sister. I was almost four years old and my sister was eight. After a short time, I saw father bring in an older woman and she was greeted by both my grandmothers with great reverence.

Mother came to me and took my hand, "Come Hagir, come get your presents."

I was taken to one of the beds where several gave me money and other gifts. I thought this was great fun, but then, my grandmothers took over and placed me on the bed that had been covered with plastic. While they removed my clothes, everyone began singing. As the singing became louder, two pinned me down to the bed and I became scared. The old woman father had brought leaned over me. My screams drowned out their singing. I never saw the razor blade she hid in her hand. The elements of speed and surprise were vital to the circumciser who pinched the clitoris between her fingers. Quickly, she held up a bloody piece of skin. Both of my grandmothers nodded their approval that enough had been removed. Then, she followed with the labia minora, stopping short of the notorious Pharaoh cut – it was over. They had done me first; as the youngest, they feared if I saw what they did to Nagla, I would fight them, and it would be much more difficult. They were absolutely right.

I remember the pain, the blood and how it made me feel at that time. As a kid, I didn't understand what they were doing or why. I remember everyone else was happy, continued singing and giving us money during the ceremony. Despite my tears and cries for help, the ceremony continued as planned by the elderly women. Bandages were placed to stem the blood flow; I was dressed as I was still crying violently and in shock. I was moved to another bed and the two women who had been holding my older sister to keep her from fleeing, forced her to the position on the bed. I remember her screams well. I can't imagine her terror as she watched me being mutilated and was old enough to know that she would soon receive the same torture.

I was not quite 4 years old, but still, I remember everything so clearly. That night in bed there was still much blood and a severe burning sensation. I reached down and brought back my hand covered in blood. I reached out beyond my bed and drew a line on my sandy wall with my own blood. My young mind just wanted to remove the entire area to stop the pain. I went and washed the area with water to relieve the burning sensation but it didn't help. The pain continued for days; I don't remember exactly when it stopped, but it finally did. After that, I wiped it from my mind for years. I never spoke about it – even with my sister who had the same experience. The first side effect came with onset of menstruation. Each period brought additional pain and frequent infections. Marriage brought painful sex and great difficulty achieving sexual arousal. Giving birth was a nightmare. I felt violated over and over again. Every wash or trip to the bathroom was a constant reminder of that violation. It definitely affects my confidence when it comes to intimacy and is a major hit to my self-esteem.

Since my parents were not particularly religious, this was not so much a matter of following a religious tenet but rather, one of culture and custom. Indeed, not having it done was considered to bring shame on the family. My father was against this extreme practice, but was under great pressure from both his mother and mother-in-law. Finally, it boiled down to them making it clear to him that it was going to happen – just a matter of when and what type.

Some explanation of the procedure is required. Essentially, there are three types (or steps) to the procedure. Type 1 is the basic Clitoridectomy. The clitoris is partially or completely removed. Type 2 is the Excision. The Labia Minor and often the Labia Majora are partially or completely removed. Type 3 is the Infibulation (known often as "Pharaoh"). This is where the labia is cut and repositioned and sewn together to make the vaginal opening much smaller. The clear intent of type 3 is to make sex impossible prior to deflowering the virgin bride after marriage while type 1 and 2 are to ensure that the female will get minimal sexual gratification – the theory being that the girl would be unlikely to wander from her marriage due to sexual desires. The WHO (World Health Organization) also recognizes a Type 4 where additional mutilation and torture such as piercing and burnings sometimes occur.

As I found out, some years earlier these same grandmothers had waited for father to be out of town and had descended on my family and had the full dreaded Pharaoh Cut performed on my older sister. Father was furious and it was the pressure of this horrid memory that weighed heavily on him.

As much as father was against it, the demands of society – especially from his own mother and mother-in-law – caused him to waiver, as they threatened to do the FULL Pharaoh Cut circumcision again, on his remaining two daughters… which would include all three types including Infibulation. Since that final step was known to cause the most damage and often required surgery later in life just to successfully have children, a movement has gained momentum in some areas where the professional "cutters" sign an oath promising not to agree to type 3 Infibulation. To avoid this, he agreed to allow the ceremony as long as he could hire a cutter who had agreed to never do Infibulation. "Cutters" were almost always elderly women. He found this woman in nearby Kosti and brought her to our house to perform the ceremony, avoiding the threats from his mother and others to do far worse damage to his daughters.

My sister and I received a combination of Type 1 and Type 2 for which we were supposed to be thankful??? To bring this horrible practice into a clear picture, the WHO estimates that there are 140,000,000 women alive today who have been subjected to this mutilation – most done between birth and puberty. Before too many Americans get comfortable with this figure knowing that most are in Africa or The Middle East, they also estimate 513,000 of these existing females have had it done in the U.S.A. where it is illegal although still done both for religious and cultural reasons. It is done by the thousands in Michigan alone. I would be remiss if I didn't point out that some would justify this barbarism as being "justified religious practices". Nowhere is it specified in the Koran or any other writings of legitimate religious affiliations that these children should be so damaged for life – both physically and mentally. It was translated and interpreted by some sick people to justify inhuman behavior. The masses seem to be more willing to follow even such perverse practices when you convince them that it is a religious requirement. It is not; it is a cultural precedent that has gone on for centuries and needs to be stopped and labeled as what it is – **child abuse.**

I didn't understand the consequences of this crime until I grew up. I didn't understand how my mom allowed this to happen. I still don't believe how someone can feel happy about putting a three and eight-year old through this experience and feel validated by hearing their pain in the form of crying for help. When you are that young, the sense of security and trust is most important, and when you lose that… you lose more than a part of your body. Moreover, they make you believe that you are dirty and that your body isn't yours – that you should feel ashamed that you were born as a woman. I don't know how it's possible that I didn't resent my mother and grandmother, but again, after the pain stopped, life returned to a new normalcy. You were forced to believe that this is a normal occurrence and a healthy one at that. They made you believe that this is just like going to school and getting medicine or even showering. It is NORMAL to do, so you don't think anything bad of it until you are old enough to know that you were a victim and that your life will never be the same and your body will never be complete.

But when I grew up, I realized that we lived in a country where female oppression is a normal occurrence. My mom was oppressed and she didn't know any better. She was raised to obey her parent's commands and follow their guidance without questioning any of their requests or actions. As a woman in Sudan, it is not unusual to not have a voice. It is not unusual to follow blindly a tradition that hurt you and your kind. It is not unusual to not think for your own body and needs but rather, follow the tradition without questioning it. When you have an uneducated group of people, you can control their movements and their actions. Most of the women my mom's age were deprived of learning. They were taught what they needed to know to take care of the men in their lives. They learned how to cook, clean and at the end of the day get ready for your husband to do whatever he pleased with your body just like he did whatever he pleased with your life. I was sad for a short period of time when I thought of the idea that my mom didn't stand up to her mother and protect us, but then, I remembered she simply didn't know any better. She needed protection herself back then, and her mother failed her just as her grandmother failed her mother. It is a vicious cycle, and unfortunately, there is no way of breaking it without a group effort and education.

Up to this day, many women believe in this ritual and practice it. Some don't just practice it but defend it. I can't wrap my head around it. I can't imagine how someone who's been through it all and suffered from the aftermath of this crime will continue to expose their kids and any other girls for that matter to this life-long suffering. Some people follow traditions blindly and some try to make it sound better by adding a religious title to it. But you can't sugar-coat this. It is a crime and a mutilation. To go along with those who claim religious freedom, they often refer to Male Circumcision and ask, "How can you allow the cutting of little boys and say that Female Circumcision is mutilation?" First, the frequency of male circumcision is dropping as more feel it's unnecessarily invasive. However, after several thousand years, the facts are irrefutable – complications are very rare and there can be medical benefits including fewer infections and possibly even a lower cancer risk. Also, it is highly likely that the removal of male foreskin actually improves sensitivity and heightens sexual success.

Again, before we get comfortable here in the United States, just recently (November 2018) this argument and other legal fights were used in an appeals case of a female doctor, Dr. Jumana Nagarwala in Detroit, Michigan whose clinic said they performed the religious ritual of female circumcision. Children were being brought to her in the Detroit area from all over the north central United States where they were submitted to FGM. This landed her in jail and put her medical license in jeopardy. Before you say, "Good riddance, she got what was coming to her" I must tell you that the appeals court declared the Federal law against FGM unconstitutional and agreed with the claim that it was basically a religious belief and therefore, protected by the constitutional right of freedom of religion. The judge also found other defects with the law. She was set free and is back mutilating young, impressionable, pre-pubescent, American born, precious little girls. The Federal Government is appealing to a higher court. We wish them success. It's interesting that this is mothers and grandmothers mutilating their female children and females doing the mutilation. Hundreds of years of tradition and beliefs will be difficult to overcome, but we must continue to force the governments of the world to protect our children.

It should be noted that unlike male circumcision, FGM on the other hand, has no medical benefit and is only done to follow a practice that some sick, sadistic man over fifteen hundred years ago thought of to supposedly make sure a wife remained faithful to her "arranged" husband and didn't find the temptation of pleasurable sex too much to resist. This was aggravated by the appearance or even the faint suggestion that the bride might not be virginal was considered enough to void the marriage agreement and require the return of the all-important dowry. This was the basis of expanding the mutilation of female children to include infibulations making virginity obvious and unquestioned. Further the World Health Organization advises that the following is proven:

Immediate complications can include:

Severe pain

Excessive bleeding (hemorrhage)

Genital tissue swelling

Fever

Infections e.g. tetanus

Urinary problems

Wound healing problems

Injury to surrounding genital tissue

Shock

Death

Long-term consequences can include:

Urinary problems (painful urination, urinary tract infections)

Vaginal problems (discharge, itching, bacterial vaginosis, infections)

Menstrual problems (painful menstruations, difficulty in passing menstrual blood, etc.)

Scar tissue and keloid

Sexual problems (pain during intercourse, decreased satisfaction, etc.)

Increased risk of childbirth complications (difficult delivery, excessive bleeding, caesarean sections, need to resuscitate the baby, etc.) and increased newborn deaths

Need for later surgeries: for example, the FGM procedure that seals or narrows a vaginal opening (Type 3) needs to be cut open later to allow for sexual intercourse and childbirth (deinfibulation). Sometimes genital tissue is stitched again several times including after childbirth, hence the woman goes through repeated opening and closing procedures, further increasing both the immediate and long-term risks

Psychological problems (depression, anxiety, post-traumatic stress disorder, low self-esteem, etc.)

Health complications of female genital mutilation

From an early age, women face FGM as a way to keep them from feeling any normal sexual arousal. Some used it to reduce a woman's libido thinking this will make her resist extramarital sexual acts – not thinking or not caring about the consequences. The inhumane practice is done to make it painful to have sex outside of marriage and to assure the man that his future wife will remain a virgin until the time comes for them to marry. The procedure intentionally alters the female genital organs without any medical reasons or health benefit. It causes the multitude of problems listed up to and including potentially being fatal. It has different forms of mutilation, partial or total removal of the external female genitalia, basically removing the clitoris, the labia minora, and in some cases, they cause narrowing of the vaginal opening through the creation of a covering seal. They form the seal by cutting and repositioning the labia minora or labia majora, sometimes through stitching the area. I don't think they thought of the aftermath of the pain that would come after you get married. Or maybe they simply didn't care. This painful practice adversely impacts girls both mentally and physically and is often performed in an unsanitary way that can also lead to infection and, in many cases, death.

I have spoken publicly about this issue; I have joined other human rights organizations whose goal is to end a culture of ignorance, but unfortunately, it continues since this practice is viewed as normal. That is why education is vital to breaking the cycle, and women are the key to ensuring that this practice ends. They are the ones who perform the procedures, so they need to stand up for their right to have a complete, untouched body and the freedom to embrace their sexuality. FGM not only promotes violence against women starting at an early age but also results in humiliation, the destruction of self-esteem and the notion that women exist only to please men. How do women recover from this experience when the scars serve as a reminder every time they use the bathroom, menstruate, make love, or give birth? How do they feel complete?

FGM is just one of many unhealthy societal practices that girls and young women are forced to bear. Other areas include being forced to marry at a very young age without the benefit of an education or the freedom to work without the approval of a male relative in some areas. We still have a long way to go to achieve equality and receive better treatment. That's why awareness and education are vital to the health and success of our society.

My mom was taken out of school, deprived of her right to education and a healthy future. She is not an only case or even a unique one. Many women back then (and now) were considered as sex objects, and their only job was to take care of the household needs, give birth and give pleasure to their man. They are not allowed to choose, complain or even speak their minds. Many were forced into an arranged marriage at a very early age, sometimes as very young children, and they didn't know any better than to say yes or worse, simply were not allowed to say anything at all.

Another bad memory I had from my early days in Sudan was the normalcy of sexual harassment from any man on the street. Riding public transportation was a nightmare. Men would come close to you and rub their genitalia or just stand too close – to the point that you feel violated. I remember one time that happened to me and I turned around and slapped that animal in his face so hard it put him in complete shock. To my surprise, other people on that transportation saw what he was doing or trying to do and said nothing and did nothing. But when I took a stand, I became the enemy. Some people were saying it was because of the way I dressed. Others were thinking it and some were questioning women leaving their house at all. Blaming the victim is a mentality that I notice often when it comes to female victims. This incident wasn't unique. It happens every day to women all over the world, and we continue to ignore how that affects us. The harassment doesn't have to be just touching you. It could be by using words, looks and/or making you feel uncomfortable in some way. Our society will never change if they keep the mentality of "it didn't happen to me personally so why should I care?" We also can't change the way we view women until we change the mixed messages that we send and the double standard that we raise our kids with. Those are just a few of the many examples that we as women face on a daily basis.

I learned later on that my father was livid about everything he was forced into that day and regretted it up to the day he died. I know he held the utmost respect for my mother and her family. He would never cross the line or become mean or violent regardless of the situation. I can only imagine how he must have felt. Although he never showed me or spoke about this with me, but deep inside, I think he realized what was done, was done and there is no going back. No undoing what was done to me and my sister – no erasing either of our memories. Life goes on.

Chapter 7

The Family

It's hardly a secret that our "being" is the total sum of our interactions with our entire family. In my case, I was fortunate to have been indoctrinated with equality, morality and respect for all by not only my parents, but all of my older siblings. As the proverbial "surprise" some five years after the birth of their 12th child, I remained close to Nagla – only five years older, but with so many older siblings, I was the combined efforts of my parents and a multitude of brothers and sisters. Indeed, Rashid – the oldest surviving son born over twenty years before me in 1955 – was more like a second father than big brother.

Parents: Seed Ahmed Elsheikh and Buthina Ibrahim

Salwa (F) (died at one year old)

Rashid (M)

Adel (M)

Twins (M) Shukri & Huseen (Huseen died at seven months of age)

Sami (M)

Haidar (M)

Nagat (F)

Husham (M)

Amal (F) (died as a teenager at fifteen years old)

Diaa (M)

Nagla (F)

Hagir (F)

I've already spoken of Amal's passing at some length. I should mention that I'm told that Salwa seemed to have a very bad case of stomach flu. Even with medical treatments available, the diarrhea and dehydration were devastating, and despite the availability of medications and intravenous therapy, they were unable to save her. Both twins also seemed healthy at birth. However, at seven months, Huseen who was still breast-fed and seemed healthy began two days of constant screaming and obvious pain. He passed away on the third day. They simply did not have the proper ability or testing machinery to diagnose his obviously severe, internal medical issue. This lack of proper medical care – even in the family of a medical professional – speaks volumes about the state of medical treatment and diagnostics available in general within Sudan and more directly, the extremely high infant mortality rate because of it.

As a young man, father was forced to move around the country. Due to this, their large group of siblings was each born in a multitude of far-reaching locations. Technically, as a medical man, he was employed by whatever hospital he worked for at the time, but the government kept a tight control over the hospitals and imposed regulations and demands which became the rule. Recognized early as a union sympathizer and organizer, he was targeted by the powers that be. Fortunately, instead of arresting him (or worse), they simply dealt with the problem by moving him frequently to many underdeveloped, distant and more remote states – many in the poor and desperate Darfur region. His transfers were dictated, not voluntary. This was simply meant to minimize his ability to cause them problems by never leaving him in one area long enough and moving him away from his base area and extended family. However, this simply allowed the cause of freedom and proper treatment of the workers to spread further by moving the message along from village to village with father and those like him. What the government thought was punishment simply spread the quest for basic human rights throughout the country – even into the remotest regions.

***

The final birth location was my childhood home in Tandalti. With so many older siblings and wonderfully involved parents, it's not surprising that I was precocious. I was a very talkative and humorous child – a real entertainer. My siblings would sometimes dress me up and make me dance and sing for them. I would even stuff newspapers down my shirt to make breasts and put on older sister's high heeled shoes to complete my Hollywood entertainer image. As the baby of so many, it seems I received more than my share of attention from all.

Mother tells me stories often of what it was like to have such a precocious little one who scared everyone by acting so much older than her years. One story she loved happened often when I was only three. As was often the case, infants were breast-fed for much longer than is normal in America. Never forgetting anything I heard, it became obvious that some of mother's friends had recently had a discussion in my earshot about my being too old for breastfeeding.

I walked into the room where mother was visiting with a couple of her friends. I was hungry, so I went to an empty chair near her and managed to half drag, half carry it to the door way. I looked at her and said:

"Buthina, I need you here for a minute." I had my arms folded and was very demanding.

Shocked at being called by name, she came to the door and leaned down towards me, "It's mother to you young lady, and what do you need my little one?"

"I'm hungry and I need to breastfeed away from your friends so they don't have to sit there and complain that I'm too old!" Laughter filled the doorway and after mother went to her friends and repeated quietly what had just happened, the laughter grew in joined in intensity.

Another time I accidentally embarrassed my parents was when we attended a wedding of a friend of my father. There are things a five-year-old is just not supposed to notice, but I wasn't your normal five year old. The groom was quite short and his new wife was tall and thin. I looked at both of them in precocious wonder.

In front of everyone, I walked over to the groom and tugged on his shirt.

He smiled and looked down at the little pre-school princess whose long, thick hair made her appear almost doll-like, "What can I do for you my sweet little one?"

I gave him my most innocent cherub-like smile. "Sir, did you stand on a stool to ask for your wife's hand in marriage?" Considerable laughter came from those in earshot, but my parents – I'm afraid – were very embarrassed, fearing the man would assume I had overheard that from the adults. Naturally, it was just me... being ME! I had come up with that strictly from my observations all on my own.

Another time, we were home and my older brother said, "We have company."

Mother went to the door and saw Nagat walking toward the door with two of her teachers – each holding one of the young girl's hands. "My goodness, what on earth has Nagat gone and done now?"

She opened the door and welcomed the teachers, shook their hands and offered them seats. "And what has Nagat done to deserve this visit?" she asked with some concern.

One of them smiled relieving some of mother's concerns. "Nagat hasn't done anything wrong. As a matter of fact, she's a delight in class. However, all we hear about is her little sister, Hagir. She claims that Hagir helps her with her homework and is very smart. We had to come and see for ourselves if there was any truth to her stories. Surely, everything she has told us can't be from this sweet little angel?" She smiled at me who by now, had come and taken mother's hand – partly out of curiosity, part fear that I'd done something wrong when I heard my name.

Mother smiled at Nagat. "Nagat darling, what would you like Hagir to do for your teachers?"

She came to me and whispered directions in my ear. I laughed realizing this would be fun and ran into the other room and got a stick we had been using the night before when we were playing. I came back into the room, walked to the table in front of the women and pounded the stick on the table.

Sternly in my best teacher's voice, "Now Nagat, I want you to learn this poem." I immediately put my hands on my hip and recited the poem that had been part of last night's homework from memory.

When I was done, Nagat tried to repeat it but messed up one line. I pounded the stick again. "Now, get it right or I'll have to send a note home to your mother."

Both women applauded and laughed loudly. One asked, "How long did it take her to memorize that?"

Nagat answered, "She just heard me read it once and she remembers it. She remembers everything she hears."

"Oh my, we do have quite a child prodigy here. What else does she do?"

After that, Nagat had me tell a couple of my made up stories and then, sing and dance for them. They had tea with mother, and as they were leaving, I heard, "If we need an extra teacher, perhaps you could loan us Hagir, but seriously, I can't imagine what we're going to do with her once she starts school. Your precious baby is quite amazing."

This scene was repeated a number of times. Nagat's school teachers would come to my home just to listen to the stories one so young would create and entertain them with. My imagination was most active from the beginning and my memory even better. It allowed me to *'Climb my own clouds'* into a future full of twists, turns, tragedies and triumphs that no one could have ever predicted.

The oldest surviving sibling, Rashid was born in 1955, some twenty-two years before I joined the family in 1977. He was very important to all our family dynamics and deserves special mention. He was well respected in our family as well as the community for many reasons. You could see why he was given so much respect when you met and talked with him. He loved reading and learning about different topics from history to poetry and everything in between. His knowledge and experience in life benefited him as well as those around him. He was politically active at that time and considered one of the leaders with his role in his political party. As I grew older, he still continued to impact who I was becoming. He invested in my development and everyone in the family and taught us everything he knew or at least attempted to do so. Teaching us was one thing, and us following and listening was quite another story – after all, we were still kids!

At a very early age, his passion was directed towards human rights – obviously, he was greatly influenced by both of our parents. His closeness to father was obvious, and they even worked together as part of the Sudanese Youth Union. When other kids were reading comic books, Rashid was introduced to novels and educational material by father and his peers. The young Rashid frequently helped by serving as a lookout during union meetings and political gatherings watching out for intruders, spies and government officials. He was my parents' helper and the entire experience had a tremendous influence on him, setting the tone for his future as a leader and activist. As I think back on this, I see much of Rashid in my daughter, Malaz. They both played a very valuable role in their parent's and sibling's lives.

Because of the constant moving of the family and transfer from school to school as well as punishment for his and the family's political activism, he was secretary at a very young age of a group called the Blue Nile Student Union, Rashid missed acceptance at Khartoum University, the most prestigious in the country. Eventually, he was accepted at the Khartoum branch of Cairo University where he studied law. With so many mouths to feed, he saw the family situation as dire and after considerable argument with our parents, quit school after only a year and a half and went to work to help support the entire family. Despite incurring the wrath of our parents, Rashid never regretted doing what he felt was his obligation to the family. Eventually, he ended up working for an Airline in Khartoum where he continued the family tradition of activism and support of the workers.

Eventually, he was forced into exile in England where he received his university diploma and eventually his master's degree from City University of London thus fulfilling his promise to our father. He remains a successful businessman in London to this day. Next to my parents, I consider him to be the most influential person in my life. With the age difference, he was and is more like a second father to me. If this seems like there might be a bit of big brother hero worship here, I plead guilty – with a thankful smile.

Chapter 8

The Big Move – Fatima Ibrahim

After the FGM and losing my sister, painful experiences both mentally and physically, we stayed in Tandalti for a few more years, and I believe that as time passed and life became more difficult, my family became willing and even ready to move on. This was through the period when Rashid had been at school in Khartoum, the capital of Sudan and now, was working there. He had been helping with the support of the family and now was almost ready to start a family of his own.

I remember when he got his job in Khartoum. He would travel away from Tandalti for a while, and when he came back, he always came with gifts, toys and clothes. He worked at one of the airlines which allowed him to visit many countries. It also allowed him to find merchandise that is not available in Sudan. One of my favorite things that he would bring back from his trips was powdered milk that came with a toy inside of it. Sometimes, I would dig for the toy before anyone could finish the milk. I loved the fact that it was a different toy each time. It is funny how some silly memories can give you a warm fuzzy feeling.

He had moved to Khartoum looking for a better life, and since my dad traveled and moved to mostly areas of distress and poverty, full of the poor and underprivileged, there were not a lot of job opportunities for Rashid to begin a career. So, he moved to the city of Khartoum and after leaving university, started working there for the airline. The family visited Khartoum twice: once for Rashid's engagement party and once for his wedding. I was very young and have little memory of those events.

Some years later, Rashid made the move to leave Tandalti decision much easier for my parents. Father had no problem finding work at a nearby hospital, and with Rashid's help, my parents were able to get a rental house from one of his friends in the city of Al Barari, very near Khartoum, which of course, is the capital of Sudan. We stayed there for three years before relocating to another suburb, Bahari where we took over Rashid's home after he was forced to flee the country. As I said earlier, Rashid was not just our older brother; basically, he was our second father. He helped raise us alongside my parents. He was one of the first people to teach us how to act properly, how to talk and to take care of ourselves. He used to brush and braid our hair and make sure we had everything we needed for school. He took the responsibility early on, and because he was very organized, well educated, and an all-round great human-being, we learned much from him.

When father decided that the time had come to move from this cozy village full of friendly neighbors to the much larger city of Khartoum, my mind raced with apprehensive wonder and more than a little sadness. "What was it like there? Would I be able to play outside, ride donkeys and horses and play in the sand with the villagers? What would the weather be like; would it be cold outside? More importantly, would I have playmates, or would I be isolated in a big city?" All those questions raced through my mind in an instant. Though much time has passed since then, I'm still able to remember my 7-year-old self and my apprehensions as if it was yesterday.

Would Khartoum provide the rustic, rural innocence of Tandalti? I remember once when we younger kids had found a snake and brought it into the house. I was holding the tail, but was too young to understand about snakes and was just following the lead of Nagat and some of my other siblings who were hanging on to the head. We kept pulling until the snake appeared unconscious. It was great fun! Big brother Haidar walked into the room and screamed to put the snake down. We of course had no idea of the potential dangers. It was left to Rashid to sit us down with a book he had on dangerous snakes and insects. As was his way, he showed us how dangerous and deadly some snakes and bugs could be and how some like our snake were harmless. He didn't yell but rather emphasized how fatal an encounter with the wrong snake could have been. It was his way to turn his worry about the dangers of exploration by two adventurous young girls into an educational opportunity. Would there be snakes in Khartoum?

All of the younger kids and I often went in search of bugs. We found many ladybugs, but there were also an abundance of beautiful and colorful varieties – no doubt, some very dangerous. We played with them all. Will there be pretty bugs in Khartoum?

Often, the older boys would wait until Father left for work. He was always admonishing us to stay away from the donkeys, worried that we would be hurt trying to ride them. But as soon as the coast was clear, they would herd several donkeys into our house. With me in the lead, we would ride the donkeys around the house for hours on end. The boys would keep watch, and as it came close to lunchtime, they would take the animals outside where father wouldn't see them and hide them until he left to return to work. Then, they were brought back inside and more hours of fun with the animals ensued. Father's concern for our safety riding the beasts of burden was overcome simply by not riding them outdoors – we rode them in our house where we could never be hurt. Will they have donkeys and horses in Khartoum? Can we have fun with them inside the house as we did in Tandalti?

We had dolls to play with that were hand made by my mother. Would they travel with us to the big city? Would she make more dolls for us? Did they have dolls in Khartoum?

My fear had no way of knowing that 'kids will be kids' whether in the big city or the rural desert. Kids will always make their own fun – just in different ways, but at this time, my young brain was most apprehensive as we prepared to leave Tandalti.

The villagers were sad to see us go and lined up to bid their goodbyes. I remember their forlorn faces, filled with tears as they handed us tokens of their affections, handcrafted items to remember them by. They may have been poor, but they were certainly rich in kindness, and of course, they were losing their "Elhakeem". Their gifts were crafted with love and they touched our hearts. That day I sobbed. Leaving those I loved and venturing into the unknown filled me with a sense of dread. That day I cried because I didn't want to leave my friends and the people I loved. I was terrified to leave behind the only life I knew only to be surrounded by the unfamiliar – the people, places, and things that would all be foreign to me. I don't remember how long the trip was, or when I fell asleep; but when I awoke, I quickly became aware that we had arrived in a large city with nice houses and paved roads, something I had only seen on the trips to visit Rashid. The roads varied from rough to smooth, and the houses changed from humble to extravagant... at least compared to Tandalti.

Our huge house was surrounded by three garden plots. One particular plot was especially bucolic, complete with chairs made for relaxing while enjoying the soaring trees and the fragrant flowers. The other two plots were fertile and bountiful with trees bursting with lemons and dates, ripe for the picking. These were secondary issues to the friends that may have been waiting in the wings, at least to my young mind. Much to my delight, I discovered that there were plenty of children who were my age and older to keep me company, even though they didn't resemble any of my friends back in Tandalti.

Soon enough, we finally settled in, and my father or my brother Rashid registered us in a nearby school. Reunited, Rashid was now actively involved in our lives and our politics. Regardless of his busy life, he managed to prioritize and find time to participate in any family event. He lived an hour or so away from us in Khartoum Bahri with his wife and his two children at that time. We visited his house a few times, and we got to know his neighbors and developed a close relationship with his kids. I believe that was another reason the family was eager to move to Khartoum to be close to Rashid and his kids. Back then, parents' involvement in their kids' school and activities was quite rare – but my family of activists was far from ordinary. I relied on my sister Nagla, who was my best friend. She and I were, fortunately, at the same school. I felt safe knowing that I had her by my side and walked with her to and from school.

We spent three years enjoying the relative comforts of Khartoum. Although Khartoum was more modern than Tandalti, our schools and homes paled in comparison to what children in the United States have grown to expect. Heat and hot water were luxuries. We either showered with cold water or made it a point to wake up early and warm the water using mom's small coal cooking fire called a Kanoon for our shower. Our bathroom was located outside – A rustic metal door with a small opening underneath was all that was between us and the elements. The glassless "windows" allowed the cold to rush in, so there was always a sense of urgency. As for towels, there were none. We had to make do with our old cloth to dry ourselves before hastily slipping into our school clothes.

The brisk walk from the shower to the house was torturous, and I recall failed attempts at covering my ears and protecting my nose from the biting wind. Once inside, things improved considerably. I would huddle with my mother around the coal cooking fire, taking comfort in the taste of the hot Chai (tea and milk) soothing my throat and warming me from the inside.

Each morning, my mother awoke before we did, brewing us that coveted cup of Chai which she served alongside a piece of bread or a biscuit that we'd happily crunch while chatting about the issues of the day. Afterward, we would embark on what often seemed like an excruciatingly long journey to school. My sister, Nagla, and I hiked miles to school in all kinds of weather – like the postman, nothing kept us from our appointed rounds, neither heat, nor cold, nor rain nor wind kept us from reaching the destination to pursue our education.

Summers were particularly challenging with little protection from the scorching sun and no water along the way to allay our dehydration. And, it's not as if we could look forward to a drink when we arrived at school. With water not readily accessible, then, sodas and juices were a luxury option to the few who could afford them – a group to which we did not belong. I should mention that water was only available in a few random locations from rustic faucets. A few more affluent people might have a Zeer either in their home, for their children at school or both. The zeer is a traditional Sudanese storage jug made of a double layer of baked clay lined with wet sand. This device is a natural cooling agent working through an evaporative system and is used to store drinking water and sometimes food. Those fortunate to have zeers at home will often place them outside their homes for thirsty people who might be passing by to drink from. These would have a small metal jug attached for this purpose. Everyone drank from the same jug. It is unsanitary but sanitation is not the first concern when someone is dehydrated. These generous neighbors created an oasis in the poor areas. Finally, it was possible to have your water tested by filling 50 ml tubes and bringing them to the laboratory at the Microbiology Department of the University of Medical Sciences and Technology in Khartoum.

Winter wasn't any better; I shiver even now when I recall how cold and dry it was. When people think of Africa, they don't think of harsh winters, but that was and is the reality. As we made our way to our destination, it wasn't unusual for the cold, almost icy, wind to pierce our skin to the point where even our faces cracked. The fact that we lacked appropriate clothing didn't help matters. There were no jackets, hats or gloves. We used Vaseline in an effort to protect our skin, but it hardly staved off the cracking and bleeding. We were expected to bear those hardships and show up on time, regardless of the weather. That's simply the way it was in Sudan during that time.

Once inside the school building, there was little respite from the elements. Classrooms lacked heat and the aging metal windows, fraught with cracks, barely kept the wind at bay. We felt every bit of it but managed to overcome our hardships and maintain our focus. Focusing wasn't always easy with what we were up against. There was no such thing as a hot meal at school. Lunches were expected to be prepared at home, so you consumed what you could afford. Some women cooked in their homes and were permitted to visit the schools and sell the meals to the students who could afford it. The meals that these women would prepare didn't vary much and mostly consisted of sandwiches made with Falafel or eggplant salad. A famous Sudanese dish called 'Fool', prepared with cooked fava beans, spices, and sesame oil was another food that was served between two pieces of bread and offered for breakfast. The same meals were served day in and day out. Meat (of any kind) was virtually unheard of for lunch. Sometimes the rich children would bring it to school if their parents had the financial means to pack it, but otherwise, it was usually saved for family meals. Those who were unable to afford to bring or buy lunch had no choice but to go hungry unless a classmate offered to share. There were no rules or regulations regarding students needing a lunch and certainly no free meal plan; the government didn't care if you ate or not.

I made friends and took the initiative to participate in sports and extracurricular activities despite the hardships. Life may have been difficult, but it was all we knew, so we tried to make the best out of it.

During my school years in Khartoum, I developed an interest in poetry and joined the literary assembly. Each morning, after the national anthem, we would be required to read a poem and talk about issues before we began our school day. With my outgoing personality and my extracurricular activities, I never found it too difficult to make friends. My brother Husham penned poems which I memorized and performed during morning assemblies. This would prove to be an important step in my development as a spokesperson and a leader later on. Not only was performing these poems a passion and a pastime for me, but it also helped me gain confidence to stand in front of people and speak.

Husham's love of poetry was contagious, and I soon learned to love poetry as much as he did. This mutual love brought us closer together. When I performed his poems during our morning assemblies, I never lost sight of the fact that he was the writer and I was his voice. As I reflect back, I realize that around this time people began to respect my views and look to me for direction. I thrived in this environment, reveling in my role as a mentor for the general student body.

One activity that I really became passionate about was playing volleyball. At first, I didn't recall any prior knowledge of the game, and there weren't many sports that girls were permitted to play. I joined the school team solely because I wanted to play a sport. I was adventurous and wanted to try something new, and volleyball was one of the few things available to me. Even though I wasn't the tallest, I was still relatively good, and the coach constantly pushed me and encouraged me to try harder. During my time on the team, I learned to love all aspects of it and proceeded to play competitively from elementary school until ninth grade when I was asked to attend a selective volleyball camp to play for the national team; I was one of around 50 or 60 in the beginning. We competed as a group until the numbers were dwindled down according to skill. In the end, I failed to make the team, but I did manage to continue until the final selection. I was disappointed of course, for not making the team but also proud to make it that far. I like to keep a positive attitude about anything that happens to me. I realized from an early age that there are many things outside of my control, and in order for me to be happy, I need to not allow the negativity to control and ruin my life. Even though I didn't play again, my love for the game didn't die at that moment. I continued playing for fun every chance I could get.

During my Elementary and middle school years, I saw many students get a beating from the teachers for simple mistakes. It wasn't an uncommon occurrence. As a matter of fact, during the morning assembly they had a routine of inspecting the student's clothing, and if they were dirty or not neatly ironed, you would get humiliated in front of everyone and get your share of whippings. The teachers could be very rough with the students. I saw many instances of severe beatings and violations of what we would think were the basic rights of the students. Often, very harsh punishment was given for the simplest mistakes.

Some teachers used the back of the ruler and some went so far as to use the metal part of the ruler and hit the back of your hand, basically your bony area which hurt worse. Some got whipped on their behind, and some got it on the bottom of their feet, their back – you name it. The teachers had the authority to punish you for anything and everything, and you couldn't do or say anything about it. You just took it and moved on. I was never a recipient of one of those beatings which they did in front of the whole school; they

54

made sure we all witnessed it. The young kids would be forced to line up voluntarily to await punishment. This was very damaging to young developing young minds and destroyed any self-esteem these poverty-stricken children might have left. Child Abuse is a part of their educational system.

The first and last time I was the recipient of a physical punishment in elementary school wasn't for a mistake that I had made, but rather, it was for my haircut. I was beat by one of my teachers because I had gotten a haircut, and she said I looked like a boy. As a young girl, I had very thick hair and it was very hard to manage. I used to cry every time my siblings or my mom washed and combed my hair, and it was just a miserable time for me. My mom refused to cut my hair; she liked long hair. It was one of the items that were just expected back then (and there). It is a beauty mark and tradition to have long hair, and women were indoctrinated into this cultural stereotype that they had to follow. My brother Rashid was there one night to see this painful experience, and I remember him trying to reason with my mom. Then, he finally took a pair of scissors and cut my hair unevenly and said to our mother, "There, now you'll have to let her get it fixed now or leave her looking like this. Thanks to Rashid, I finally got my hair cut very short. The next day when I went to school my teacher saw it and thought it was inappropriate for a girl to have hair that short, like a boy, she said. She penalized me severely for that. I remember it vividly even though I was so young. She pinched me in the stomach so hard that she was able to lift my small thin body completely off the floor by just two fingers. Her long nails dug into and cut my skin. Then, she took a metal edged ruler to the back of my hands where there is nothing but skin and bones. She kept hitting over and over; I can still feel it today. I will never forget how her verbal admonishments and severe punishment made me feel.

In spite of those terrible memories and hardships, life was much simpler all the way up to high school. People seemed friendly and involved in each other's life. I am not sure if I liked it back then, but I definitely remember how safe I felt. In the neighborhood, we were safe and protected and played until the street lights came on; that was our cue to return home. In our neighborhood and all throughout Sudan, people trusted one another. Neighbors were there to correct us if we made a mistake and protect us from any danger. Our neighbors, siblings, and the people we surround ourselves with are how we grow and develop as people. We laughed and slept peacefully. Remembering this and thinking about how hard it is for me to fall asleep and stay asleep, now makes me wonder – *is it harder to have a difficult life but enjoy peace of mind, or the opposite?*

***

My life was progressing. I was growing and developing as a young woman and all seemed well, but sometimes, things can be too good to be true. Before long, you're lulled into a false sense of security. When I was twelve or thirteen, my father picked my brother Diaa and me to teach how to give injections and even start IV's. Many of father's patients began to ask for Diaa or me to give them injections as they said we had gentle hands, and they didn't even feel the injections. It seemed as if life had finally stabilized and all was calm, peaceful and going well. Little did I know that my life was about to be shaken to the core.

My family was involved in the politics of Sudan which helped me understand life and politics. It didn't take long for me to become passionate about it. The knowledge that my family filled me with enabled me to become an activist and helped me mature as a leader.

For the majority of my early childhood, Gaafar Nimeiry served as the president of Sudan. He was a dictator who killed many activists

56

after he came to power in 1969 from a military Coup. So, many changes happened during his time as a president that led to the revolution in 1985. After that, Sudan enjoyed a short-lived freedom. I was only eight years old at that time. Unfortunately, those four years came to an end, and a rogue military coup overthrew our democratic government in 1989, forcing Sudan into a dictatorship, yet again, and it is still present to this very day. The coup wreaked havoc on the country and before we knew it, everything was descending into chaos.

Prior to the 1989 coup, our house served as a gathering place where speakers and leaders of the Democratic Forefront congregated to work on their campaigns. When I reflect back on those times, I am reminded of one day in particular. My family hosted an event which attracted many prominent leaders. Out of all the people who attended, a very strong, tall, inspiring woman dressed in white traditional Sudanese wear called "Al tob", stands out like a shining light in the dark recesses of my memory. Her name was Fatima Ibrahim. (no relation to mother) I remember as I sat in the front listening to her, that I didn't quite understand what she was saying at that time, but it sounded real to me. After listening to her speech, seeing how people reacted to her words, I knew she was someone special. That was the moment she became my idol. It was later in life that I had the privilege to learn she truly is an amazing woman.

After delivering a resounding speech to much applause in our front yard, I approached her to say hello, and she bent down and softly planted a kiss on my cheek. Each time I relive that heartfelt moment, I smile. It was then that I remember aspiring to be like Fatima – to make a difference and influence people. Fatima's husband was slain at the hands of President Nimeiry many years prior. It shaped her and made her purpose even stronger. My father greatly admired her intelligence, strength, and resilience.

When I grew older, I learned how powerful Fatima was and the impact she had, not just on Sudan, but on Africa in general. She placed herself at the forefront, advocating and fighting for women's rights and human rights in Sudan and globally. In her twenty's, she helped lead a revolution in Sudan and would later become the first woman in Parliament and the first Sudanese woman deputy of Parliament not only in Sudan but in all of Africa and the Middle East. Fatima grew up in a family just like mine – politically aware and active in their communities. Fatima had a wall (underground) newspaper called Elra'edda meaning "Leading or pioneer Girls". The topics focused on women's rights issues, democracy and the oppression of colonialism.

Fatima organized the first women's strike in Sudan because the administration in her school decided to cancel science classes and replaced them with family science classes. The strike was successful. She founded the Intellectual Women's Association, and she was one of the founders for the Sudanese Women's Union where she served on the executive committee and later became the president. Fatima was also the chief editor of the Woman's Voice Magazine (published by the Women's Union). She also became a member of the first Sudanese Party which had an internal women's structure. Fatima was later placed under house arrest for several years and arrested many other times during the Nimeiry regime. To put it simply, without women like Fatima fighting with all that they had to give us a voice and the ability to stand tall and fight for our rights at that time, I don't know where we would be today or where would I be.

***

Life changed after the coup. The government began silencing and torturing dissenters, forcing many to leave the country. Before this fateful time, I was attending elementary school and thinking of how inspiring the people were and how peaceful the future seemed. This comfort lasted but a short time and life grew increasingly difficult as the government started dictating all aspects of our lives. They told us what to wear, when to speak, and how to live. It was a grueling time, to say the least. We lost so many of our citizens to torture during this horrendous period.

My oldest brother, Rashid, was forced to leave the country after he was let go from his job for political reasons, as were many other activists. He realized that staying would put his life at risk. Life as my family knew it had taken a drastic turn, and we all could see the concern in my father's eyes. To see the man whom we adored in such pain, just ripped at our hearts.

My older sister, Nagla, was attending high school at the time and was politically involved there; I followed her lead and began attending meetings and becoming active in my community as well. It all seemed to make sense – participating in peaceful rallies and speaking to students. Before long, we were becoming stronger and more organized. We had to overcome many trials because our schools were segregated by sex, but we still managed to make it work.

Chapter 9

High School – A Rebel Comes Forward

I later attended Bahari El Jadida High School where I was very active. In Middle School, we were required to wear brown uniforms, but now we wore a sky blue long dress that went below the knees as well as long pants underneath to be certain we didn't show too much. Now that we were older and past puberty, we were required to wear a headscarf and always have it with you – or be punished severely. However, I chose to just have mine on my shoulders, which serves the purpose of looking fashionable as well as clearly demonstrating my political views. I was in the poetry art club as well as the drama club. As a leader, I helped bring in outside entertainment to the school – singers, dancers and theater people brought the outside world into this all-girl High School.

I had many friends both in and out of school. I related well with Nagla's friends even though they were several years older. I was mature for my age and was able to hold my own in any intellectual conversation. I had one close friend who was already studying Art in college. She introduced me to those in the college community where I met many who were intelligent and concerned about "making a difference in the world" and causing change, but they did know how to enjoy life in spite of their political struggles: the wars, the tortures and the hardships all of that brought to everyday life in Sudan.

This time brought my first crush. I spent many evenings with these older friends and one artist became very close. It was obvious that we really liked each other, but we never actually discussed it or admitted our feelings – or acted on them physically. I just enjoyed the conversations and the feelings I experienced being with him. One day, he fled the country leaving me with a great feeling of loss. I had a very difficult time dealing with the sudden separation, and even though this wasn't a committed relationship in any way, I just knew that we both had deep down feelings for each other. After this loss, I kept everything to myself and didn't discuss it with anyone, but I did write poems and short stories about it which gave me my first experience with writing. I wouldn't say that my first works were very good, but they were real and very expressive – an emotional release I very much needed. After those early writings, I discovered that writing can be therapeutic and my first diary was born.

An interesting aside is that twenty-two years later I located this first passion on social media and we had an excellent conversation about our past which confirmed that our feelings were mutual back then. It was a very good walk down memory lane with him, and we both agreed that we made choices back then that were dictated by a multitude of factors. But, we did have feelings toward each other that were very real. However, we both knew that the past was in the past.

All of this experience with older and more active college people solidified my ability to be a leader in High School, and I became even more politically aware. I would speak out and help in organizing and participating in peaceful rallies and protests. I learned that I was willing to fight for my convictions and wasn't afraid to speak my mind for the greater good. My mouth was my greatest and most dangerous weapon. I had already established a good relationship with many of the kids in and around my school, so when I spoke, people listened. Before I knew it, word had spread about my (and many others) political involvement to the government. My family – my father in particular – completely supported me.

Of course, every action has an equal and opposite reaction. As word quickly spread, the Sudanese government began to pay close attention to the prominent political organizations and protesters. To say they weren't the slightest bit pleased that the citizens of

61

Khartoum had the courage to stand up to them, is an understatement. They began to attach severe consequences to quell uprisings, including detainment and torture. Being as politically active and determined as I was, I ended up being on the receiving end of these tactics. My political actions weren't without a cost, and I paid dearly in the form of mental and physical torture. My first experience with this was when I was detained after a peaceful rally organized by the students. Remember, I was still very young – fifteen or sixteen years of age – not a nineteen or twenty-year-old college student. We chanted against the government and demanded a better life, challenging the cost of food and the many other issues that confronted us as citizens living under a tyrannical regime. The government had the police and the army officially, but we were detained by what was called an Internal Security Unit ISU division of the NISS (National Intelligence and Security Service). You might consider them to be the "political" police. These are the henchmen of the regime – very similar to the Sharia Law "Religious Police" in other Arab States. They operate above the rule of law, but are sanctioned and directed by the government.

Interrogators demanded answers about our intentions, and when we refused to speak, we were beaten, verbally assaulted and denied water, food, and the opportunity to sit down. They forced us to stand for long hours until it was impossible to remain on our feet. At the end of the day, we were released and ordered to return early in the morning and stay for an extended period of time once again, which caused us to miss school, and of course, this detention kept us from our mission. We realized that such acts of cruelty were meant to break our will, but they merely inspired many of us to fight harder.

***

I continued to get arrested for my political activism – so many times, in fact, that I can't even recall the exact number. The government detained us in what they called "Ghost Houses," where no one could find us. It was in those houses that our captors beat us with anything they could find—wood, metal, you name it. One incident that I remember well (what an understatement; it will NEVER be forgotten) was when 1 was detained with three of my friends for a period of almost four weeks at Bahari's Ghost House. They ordered us at the office at 6 a.m. each day and kept us until 9 p.m. At this time, they were still cautious about keeping us all night. We had no choice but to go, or they would retaliate against our families. My father was there with me every day, yelling at them, and warning the authorities. Just hearing his voice was enough to keep me going. Afterward, they let us go and I went back to school and continued to help organize rallies and meetings. One night, during a particularly large rally, they came and arrested many activists, including me.

Central Square – Bahari, Sudan

A large number of young people had gathered in the central square. Most were High School students with a few older, college-aged students mixed in. Three young girls and a couple of boys were standing on a concrete wall firing up the crowd with surprising rhetoric for ones so young and even more surprisingly for females in this Islamic Society. They spoke against the government and against the President (Dictator) specifically. Conditions deteriorated rapidly and while the police were charged with dispersing the crowd, the far more dangerous ISU/NISS members quietly made their way towards the young leaders. They all tried to escape. There were many of them headed for only a handful of high school student leaders and any others trying to escape. Many managed to outrun them, but quite a few were caught by the ISU/NISS – including the three female leaders: girls who should be worrying about hair, makeup, boys,

63

music and anything other than starvation, food prices, democracy and equality for all women – were now prisoners of this group of tormentors who would show no mercy because of age or sex. They knew immediately that they should fear for their lives.

While the police dispersed the rest of the crowd, with swift efficiency, the ISU/NISS secured many and along with the three female ringleaders were all brought to one of their headquarter Ghost Houses. One man seemed to be in charge. He looked over the room full of young people. "I want those three girls kept separate – especially the thin, pretty one; that's Hagir, Seed Ahmed Elsheikh's kid. We've dealt with her way too often. Her mouth will be silenced this time, and it won't hurt to send that trouble making father of hers a message he will understand. Take them to the interrogation room," he ordered.

They were handled very roughly especially considering they were such young girls. This did not bode well for their future; the interrogation took hours. All three were beat and forced to stand with their arms over their head. If they began to relax their arms, they were beat again with a hose. They seemed to dwell on Hagir. They knew from previous experience that she would remain silent, so this time, they went right at her – beating away. They knew they couldn't break her. After a few hours of this, they tired of asking their questions again and receiving nothing but silence in return. They were beaten harder and blood was drawn – especially Hagir – their "frequent flyer" and the obvious student leader.

Across town, Elhakeem was busy at work, treating the sick and dying at his hospital. He heard a commotion only to see one of his sons running towards him.

"Father, they've got her again, but this time it looks bad. They were far rougher with her, and I fear she has pushed them past the breaking point. Sometimes, I wish you hadn't taught her so well. She's so damned young."

"Damn, I've been afraid of this. Do you know which Ghost House they've taken her to?"

Her brother was quick to answer, "No, I have no idea. Those who told me what happened were more concerned with escaping themselves. They couldn't very well follow the security forces. Those guys are quite tired of dealing with her. They know she won't speak; she won't give in to them. She will just take whatever they do to her. Their anger will show in her beatings. I don't know how much more she can take, and I fear they will try and send you and our brothers a message, too."

"OK, let's stop by the Union Office and see how many we can get to go with us. If they know we're looking for her, at the very least, they might hesitate to kill her." With that, they were off to enlist others to assist in their quest to find Hagir and the others. On previous occasions, he had been successful in finding where they had brought her, and he was able to loudly protest what they were doing to one so young. The shouting of this well-respected man and his friends had in the past at least, caused the ISU people to hesitate and perhaps ease up a bit on their torture of his youngest daughter. Certainly, it made them hesitate to go to that final, mortal solution to his daughter's constant rebellion against the government.

"Ghost House" is the term used for these unofficial headquarters of the ISU. They are the home base for interrogation, torture and murder of political activists. They function directly at the will of the Dictator and are notorious around the world. The UN continues to try and monitor them and issues papers detailing their atrocities and edicts of condemnation which of course, do nothing to stop them. These officers are not trained police or soldiers. Rather, they are thugs – little more than street gangs functioning with impunity while the police turn their backs on any other illegal activity.

The house, itself, has several detention rooms for large quantities of the persecuted. Many of these houses also have a few actual barred cells for the more physically belligerent. There is of course, the notorious interrogation room where torture is a means to an end and murder is often condoned. It is not unusual for a dissident to go into a Ghost House and disappear from the face of the earth.

Finally, one of the guards came in from outside the walled compound. They no doubt knew that her father and family were looking for her. What happened next was probably destined after so many trips to the Ghost House and everyone knowing her family history. The "thug" in charge just motioned toward the door. They knew exactly what he was ordering.

With her blood-stained, sweat-soaked blouse no longer hiding her young, post-puberty femininity, they roughly grabbed her and literally dragged her outside into the yard of the Ghost House. She now knew that her father and his friends were searching for her. She grieved just a bit knowing the pain and anguish she was causing him. Then, she actually managed a small smile. She knew that whatever they did to her, her father and family would be most proud of their youngest child, but that brief smile at that moment of pride was very short lived as they gruffly tied a rope to her wrists and threw it over the limb of a tree. She was soon dangling from her wrists, well off the ground.

With that, the thugs took turns hitting her. Whips, pipes, 2x4 boards, hoses, whatever they could find. When one person got tired of beating her, another would take his place. The guards mocked and laughed at her. She remained silent. She never called out. She just took it.

For the first time, this torture went on for over ten hours – throughout the night. She could smell her own blood; her clothes were shredded and by that time, her body was numb. She had come to the conclusion that this was probably the final episode in her young life. Around sunrise, they untied her, threw her in the back of a pickup truck. They didn't care that she had many serious injuries. They didn't care that just moving her was an agonizing ordeal. No, they just hauled her fragile, beaten and abused body toward her home.

Elhakeem's heart broke as he searched the streets for his baby. He checked headquarters and every security facility he knew of. He found no sign of his daughter or her friends. He spent much of the night just wandering the streets.

Finally, her brother looked at father, "Father, please... this is not doing any good. Let's go home and hopefully, they'll release her soon."

But there would be no sleep this night. Father got a chair and put it outside the front door to our home. Then, he sat awaiting word on his precious Hagir. He couldn't help wonder if all of the wonderful things he had instilled in his children: freedom, equality, dignity, human rights, women's rights and education for all – had he paid the ultimate price for wanting to make a difference in this world? Had he sacrificed his own child? Was this all his fault? He was consumed with grief and guilt. As the sun rose over the eastern skies, he heard the sounds of a vehicle coming down the unpaved road that went past his house. He jumped to his feet.

The driver looked at his partner next to him. "Excellent, that old fool is out in front of his house waiting for his precious daughter."

He slowed the Toyota pickup truck and never came to a complete stop. The two men in the bed of the pickup simply reached for their bloodied and severely wounded cargo. With no regard to her age, sex or condition, they simply lifted her diminutive, lifeless body and heaved it in the direction of her father – as if they were tossing a bag of trash onto the sandy ground that made up the front yard of their home.

She was only conscious enough to hear her father's voice as he carried her inside – she could remember little else. He whispered in her ear, "Be strong Hagir; I'm here; you're home; you're safe now." Buthina Ibrahim was beside herself with a mother's grief seeing her baby in such a state. As she was comforted by one of her older daughters, she remembered how little Hagir was never afraid to speak out nor was she afraid of punishment. When she would do something wrong and one of her older siblings would try and discipline her with a bit of loving corporal punishment, she would just stand there and take it – silently and without tears – staring them down. She would wait until they were done and left her alone. Only then, would she cry or touch wherever she was hurt. Thankfully, Hagir was a very good child and seldom met the wrath of the family. By the time she took on the Sudanese Government, she had already learned that for her, crying was associated with weakness – and she would NEVER be weak, no matter what they did to her.

As he stood by the bed as his wife and several of his children cared for Hagir, tears appeared again on her hardened, experienced, activist father. He could only wish that it was he who had been so severely beaten instead of his little, precocious Hagir – his youngest and brilliant daughter – the one destined to be *Climbing On The Clouds*.

***

When I woke up in my own bed, every inch of my swollen body was aching in pain. To this day when I remember these horrific incidents, I tear up. The pain was so real. I knew that fighting for what I believed in would have reactions, but I was blind to the real consequences of what they'd really do to me. I was unable to lie on my back and had no use of my right arm for over a month. I spent the entire period in bed recovering from my wounds.

One of the young boy student leaders – freedom fighters – was my partner during this protest and he had managed to escape. That next day he managed to find out where I lived and showed up to make sure I was all right. When he saw how badly I had been hurt, perhaps feeling guilty, he came by to visit my bedside every day. This brought us very close. I can't say it was love, more like comrades in arms, but I had been through a terrible experience and he provided someone I could relate to during this traumatic recovery period. We also had many mutual friends, who were rooting for us to have a relationship, but it was short lived and we moved on.

With all the activism in my family, you probably won't be surprised to learn that my brother, Haidar is a lawyer. He played a major role during those tough times with the entire family – not just me – frequently needing his services. Many times he helped guide me toward the right direction and provided me with insights. He is a very kind, sweet individual, and I grew to become very fond of him, not only as a brotherly love but also as a friend and a mentor. His quiet demeanor and wisdom were so refreshing. It helped me calm down sometimes. His jokes and upbeat personality made it so easy to enjoy life even when I was hurt.

So many of us lacked trust in the authority at that time. It was hard to find someone in a powerful position who wasn't an ally of the government. They got rid of all their opponents and anyone who disagreed with their views. If you didn't follow their way, you would either lose your job or get tortured or both. The principal of my High School was an ally of the government and refused to allow me to attend school after that last detention. He made only one conciliatory decision; he permitted me to take my final exams. However, he accused me of being a security threat because I helped organize a revolution. My father, undaunted, vowed that the punishment would not affect me. "She will return, receive the same grades she was getting before, and successfully complete her exams," he exclaimed. I subsequently, stayed home, and with the help of my friends and tutors whose names I can't reveal, I continued to excel, making my father proud with excellent grades on my final exams. I was determined to show them that they could not put me down. They could not stop me. I am and was *a force to be reckoned with.*

Despite all of the detentions and beatings, I still found it within myself to work hard on my schoolwork and still fight for a better tomorrow. To do any less would be letting them win, but I was still hurting. Much of my body was now black and blue, and I was still in considerable pain – reminding me of the recent tortures. My right arm and shoulder, especially, hurt the worst – having suffered greatly from the awkward way my arms had to hold my suspended body while hung from the limb of the tree at the ghost house, not to mention the indiscriminate beatings. Most likely, my shoulder was severely dislocated and muscles torn in addition to the bruises and wounds. It became necessary to force myself out of bed for daily lessons at home. I had to pass my final exams and get my High School diploma. One of the student teachers my father had found to come to our home did push me to the limit. After I incorrectly answered one of his questions, as Sudanese teachers were frequently likely to do, he physically hit me on the upper right arm. This was a huge mistake. My black and blue body and severely injured right shoulder and arm were in no condition to withstand this. He hadn't thought and had instinctively been physical as a learning reinforcement – as teachers were want to do in Sudan. I screamed and begged him not to do that again, as even a light tap was agonizing. He apologized and we returned to work.

However, the next day, he did exactly the same thing. My patience had been beat out of me by the government thugs. I yelled loudly at him and told him in no uncertain terms that he was no better than the government torturers, controlling by violence and that I wasn't interested in his help if "beating" was his way of teaching. He finally got the message and fortunately, continued tutoring me. Hopefully, I had broken him of the habit of teaching with physical violence.

I went on to graduate from high school with honors and was accepted at Sudan University of Science and Technology where I majored in Electrical Engineering. I had survived High School. I had survived the Government and their goons. But as Winston Churchill once said after the retreat from Dunkirk during World War II, *"This is not the end. It is not even the beginning of the end. But it is, perhaps, the end of the beginning!" - Winston Churchill.*

Chapter 10

University – The Rebellion Continues

From Poet: Martin Niemöller

First they came for the communists, and I did not speak out - because I was not a communist;

Then they came for the socialists, and I did not speak out - because I was not a socialist;

Then they came for the trade unionists, and I did not speak out - because I was not a trade unionist;

Then they came for the Jews, and I did not speak out - because I was not a Jew;

Then they came for me - and there was no one left to speak out for me."

While in college, I continued fighting along with the Democratic Forefront and continued my quest to educate and enlighten students on important issues. During this time, the government continued to gain strength. Additional rights were trampled on and even removed, and more lives were lost as they started shipping young graduates off to fight in a war between the north and the south which started way back in 1955. Some successfully fled the country; others weren't so lucky.

I would require a separate book to relate the details of the conflict between North and South that has been – and continues to be – a way of life in Sudan since 1955. It is far too complicated to properly detail it here. However, it's important to realize that it is what I shall call an ethno-religious conflict. The North (Sudan) is 97% Muslim while South Sudan is 97% Christian and indigenous religions – indeed, many of the Christians are Roman Catholic (including the current president). Most of the dramatic pictures shown around the world of starving children in Sudan are either from the South and war-torn areas or the Western Darfur region, but these starving children all have one thing in common – their only crime is being the wrong religion (at least as far as Khartoum was concerned). While the current Sudanese regime receives support from other Arab States and terrorist organizations who want Sharia Law forced on the world, to claim this as a Religious conflict would be a gross oversimplification – although, to continue this support, the government in Khartoum has imposed Sharia Law on Sudan. To show how complicated Sudan the conflicts in Sudan can be, the official languages having been a British Territory are English and Arabic, but the United Nations lists a total of 114 different languages spoken between Sudan and South Sudan. Tribal languages vary, often from city to city and state to state.

Indeed, as is so often the case, OIL complicates the issues. The border oil fields which are primarily in the South: Bentiu, Unity, Adar and Heglig, present a promise of potential wealth to Sudan too tempting to just accept the UN mandates and treaties creating the ethnic and mostly Christian country of South Sudan. Therefore, war continues to this day (despite peace treaties) and the UN tells us that more have died as a direct result of this conflict, counting since 1955 – both military and civilian – than anywhere in the world since World War II and the end of the Holocaust perpetrated by Hitler and his fanatical followers – more than Korea, more than Viet Nam, more than the Iraq/Iran war, more than Kuwait, more than the Iraq war to remove Saddam Hussein, more than Afghanistan! The Arab Sharia Countries pour in military supplies to Sudan while the current African countries south of South Sudan who supported the rebellion in 1955: Uganda, Kenya and Tanganyika continue to support the Government of South Sudan today. Unfortunately, that leaves millions of people starving and without medical support while the oil beneath their sands – a potential salvation for all – sees little mining and cultivation and most of that is being done by Khartoum as part of the peace treaties. So, a revival of this civil war and the pressures it put on all citizens, weighed heavily on myself and my fellow college students.

The University was like a small, walled city. The government wanted to control all aspects of college life, and by this time, the difference between the police and the dictator's ISU was that the ISU had deteriorated into the Religious police so prevalent in conservative Arab countries. The main entrance to the University was often guarded by these thugs. While I wore the Blue Dress uniform in high school which covered our bodies from the neck down, I had refused to cover my head or fully comply with their demeaning wardrobe demanded of women. As college students, we – as grown women – were subject to their forced compliance to these conservative ways. Of course, my persona and the word compliance never went together.

Dressed very much as any eighteen-year-old girl anywhere, I defied the government hooligans. I often played games with them at the door. They would verbally abuse me for my sacrilegious attire, but their own conservatism forbade them from physically touching a young, adult, grown woman. Often, I was able to just ignore their taunts and squeeze by their attempts to force my adherence to their beliefs.

On one occasion, the security guard managed to stop me and harass me. One of my friends joined in when he saw what was happening. He accused me of not being dressed appropriately for class and refused my entry to the University. In the end, after much shouting back and forth, it became very heated and one thing led to another. The thug felt that both I and my friend who stepped up to protect me must be punished, so he reported us to the government, and we both ended up in jail. In Sudan, there is no justice. Anyone

74

with a badge sanctioned by government officials had the power, and we were both dragged into a courtroom for arraignment where the guard accused us of attacking him. With my brother, Haidar for a lawyer and a large throng of University Students there to support us both and demand our immediate release, the security guy felt the 'insecurity' and changed his testimony and we were released. Eventually, not wanting to repeat this arrest or the Ghost House memories of my younger years, it was necessary to find a way around them.

As part of this city within a city status of the University, the professors were provided with homes for themselves and their family. These apartments (almost Condo-like) had exits both into the University area and outside into the real world. A girlfriend was the daughter of one of the professors. Often, I was able to quietly walk around to the outside entrance to her apartment, and she would let me in to where I could pass through her home to the inside entrance to the University – totally avoiding the Religious Police – and still attend classes dressed any way I saw fit. Effectively, as a girl, I had to sneak into school every day just to get the education I was determined to receive.

Throughout this period, I was still a frequent public speaker. I joined with my friends and we organized protest events and demanded such 'taken for granted' things as Peace, Human Rights, Women's Rights and a better life for all – no matter their gender or religious beliefs. Once again, these peaceful events were frequently interrupted by arrests and detentions. Many students joined our efforts and fought beside us. At that point, many families were being directly affected by the actions of their government. Unfortunately, people often don't recognize major issues until they affect them and/or their families – directly. Only then do they feel obligated to take a stand.

Our effort was aimed at trying to change this mentality and make people care about others. Compassion and love are traits that – I believe – we can teach to others. As Nelson Mandela said:

"No one is born hating another person because of the color of his skin, or his background, or his religion. People must learn to hate, and if they can learn to hate, they can be taught to love, for love comes more naturally to the human heart than its opposite."
Nelson Mandela

This embodies my purpose and my vision. This is what as a young woman in college, I tried to spread to all – and to the best of my abilities, I used peaceful protest and words of humanity to change what I saw as the wrongs of the world, but sometimes, you are cornered, and the only way out is to fight back to protect yourself.

At one point, we were forced to fight back against the government, the security teams, and the Islamic Forefront representatives in our college. We fought back; we were chased down, and many were arrested after they were caught. I was seriously injured during this clash and was bashed in the head with a metal bar. I fled with the help of some friends to a nearby street for shelter while cradling my cracked skull that was bleeding profusely. We heard someone calling us from one of the houses, and a woman opened the door and whispered to us:

"Hurry up and come in." It was in that moment that I was reminded why I was determined to continue fighting. I was reminded that I was not alone in this fight. There were many people who could not be at the forefront of the fight but were in the shadows helping those when they needed it, like the woman who helped save my life.

The residents of the house first attempted to stop the bleeding before hiding me under the bed. They had also provided me with a change of clothes. But then, I heard the telltale hard knock of the security guards. The matriarch of this home quickly ordered the family members to sit on the bed to disguise the fact that I was hiding beneath it. They then, continued to engage in casual conversation as she answered the door and informed the searchers that no one was there other than those who resided there. With a very strong voice, she denied them entrance, and swayed by her firm resistance, they left. Perhaps they respected her because she was an older lady. I am not entirely sure why they took her word for it, but I certainly was relieved that they did. I survived to fight future battles.

After the scare was over, the kind lady and her family helped me up and called my brother-in-law, Nagla's husband, Bukhary to come and get me. Bukhary was a fighter himself and understood why I persevered. He arrived after dark and spirited me off on his motorcycle down long, winding back roads where it was safe to travel – unimpeded by the still searching authorities. When I arrived home, my family helped me, but no doctor was able to tend to my head wounds – my father had to do what he could with no x-ray or higher medical assistance. When I reflect back on the kindness of the lady, the residents of that house, I realized that these small gestures gave me the strength to carry on.

After I was returned to my house, I learned that I wasn't the only one injured. Another close friend was also severely beaten, and it was made clear to all that anyone who took it upon themselves to kill us would be rewarded – effectively, we had a bounty on our heads. At that time, I was forced to leave my house and go into hiding. My sister, Nagla, and her husband helped me make the decision where to hide. We chose a close friend who was also a doctor and stayed there until things settled down.

During this time, my older brother Rashid, who was already residing in England, was a human rights activist and took the issue public in London. I believe the government was trying to avoid as much negative publicity as possible, and thanks to Rashid, they overturned my sentence *'in absentia'* and removed the bounty offered for my death. That very same day, my idol, Fatima Ibrahim called me from London and stated that she was very proud of me and that they would continue fighting for me. That phone call gave me a renewed life and the strength to push forward.

During those college years, I studied, I celebrated, I made many friends, and **rejected** all efforts to infringe upon my freedom. Some of those friends became lifelong relationships and were a profound influence on my life in many ways. I learned a lot from them, and they often gave me the courage to continue. If I wanted to talk about them individually, I would need another lifetime of time to tell you all the stories. Some of them still live in Sudan which prevents me from naming names as that same dictatorship still has control in Sudan.

Those years in college were a major turn in my life – I learned a lot and grew immensely as a human being. I found a strength and courage that I didn't know existed within me which aided me in my upcoming journey and helped me trust my abilities and survival skills. Even though I believed we could initiate changes and really make a difference in the world if we continued fighting, it seemed impossible – especially when we heard people on the street talk about activists in a degrading way and say that if we didn't want to be arrested, then, we should stay home. Many people still believed that a woman's place is at home, making babies and keeping the husband happy – not in college or working and definitely not on the street fighting for her rights. The ugly reality hit me at that moment, and I realized that as women, our existence isn't appreciated or acknowledged by society, and before we can be a part of any change, we need to correct that first. In order for women to be a part of any change or participate in any decisions, we need to have a true representation in all the discussions that affect us, and that isn't the case right now. It is a vicious cycle.

At some point, I feared for my life and the future became dark. I started to lose faith in the people, so I had to ground myself to stay positive. It wasn't easy for me to consider escaping from Sudan at that time. I had to weigh the risks of staying, and after comparing it to what I witnessed all those years, I finally decided to pack my bags and leave. With lots of help from my family and others, for my own survival, I decided to leave Sudan to go to Egypt and decide where my life would go from there.

Chapter 11

Marriage

Prior to entering college, I met a friend of my brother-in-law Bukhary whom I thought to be a kindred spirit due to the political views that we held in common. Little did I know at the time that marrying him would be a near fatal mistake.

At this point, the lawyers – for reasons that will become apparent as we continue on with my life's experiences – have told me that I can't use my soon to be husband's name. I've thought about how to handle this a great deal. Shall I just give him an appropriate name? I could just select a common Sudanese name: Kareem, Aziz, Faraj or whatever. We even discussed just calling him plain old "Fred", but this might be risking upsetting everyone named Fred who might read this unique life's story.

Dictionaries describe a Chimera as a multi-faceted Greek Mythological she-monster with the head of a lion, a goat's body and the tail of a serpent – the ultimate description of multi-personality paranoia. Like the famed Chimera, my first husband had many sides to him which my perceived love for him blinded me to. Calling him "Chimera" seems most appropriate. He had many personalities – some quite well hidden; some were quite dangerous just like a Chimera. Finally, since the Chimera was a mythological she-monster, you'll have to allow me a small, ironic smile, for very much like so many of the radicals who have devastated the land where I was born and caused so much death and suffering, in the end, he turned out to be the ultimate male chauvinist – capable of mistreating any woman who didn't submit to his domination. I apologize for this interruption. We can now move on with my extraordinary tale – my path to *climb on my own clouds*.

***

80

We met in Khartoum. Nagla and Bukhary had invited some of their friends along to a party, and since I was "mature" for my age and so close to my big sister, they asked me to join them. I had just completed high school and had been accepted at Sudan University. At this party, Nagla introduced me to her husband's friend, Chimera. He was quite charming and very pleasant to talk with. Since we had so much in common and he was so easy to talk with, I was quite taken with him. It was a very pleasant experience.

After that initial meeting, he found reasons to accompany my sister and her husband to my home for a few special events. He was quite attracted to me, and honestly, I pretty much felt the same way. He told me that he wished to have a relationship, but with everything going on in my life, my political efforts, the recent tortures and my upcoming entrance into the University, I was very hesitant. Over the course of a month, he persisted – did I mention he was VERY charming? I gave in and we were officially "dating" and in a committed relationship.

We had a very good relationship and our attachment grew – I fell in love. He wrote me lovely letters and was so expressive with his feelings. Thinking back on it; he was always there, and between Chimera's constantly being at my side and our busy political life, I missed out on much of the college life experience and probably should have dated others if for no other reason than to be able to compare. I did have other suitors during my years at Sudan University – a few I might easily have had feelings for. But, I was in a committed relationship, and as I neared the end of our college years, marriage was expected. I never strayed from my love.

At that time, I thought that this is what love should be and was thinking about building a future with this person. To be honest, there were times when I had my doubts and had moments where I wanted to call it off. I actually did call it off once, but he was very

81

convincing and I was determined to honor my commitment. Another reason to continue was because we created so many good memories in the time we spent together – there was no doubt about that. I can't say I really knew him well though, because with school and politics, we were only together for short periods of time. We were both very active politically and had very busy social lives, friends, and extracurricular activities. I continued throughout my college years to be very visible to the powers that be. There were many run-ins with the law and more than a few beatings, but none as bad as those at the Ghost House during high school – but bad enough. I was a constant aggravation to the authorities. My status was somewhere between being a pain in the ass to them and having a very large bull's eye on my back. My life and activism to date had placed my continued good health in serious question. With both of us being so active, living so dangerously, it was probably a miracle that we were able to marry with all the pomp and circumstance the occasion deserved.

***

The sound of the Daloka's traveled throughout the neighborhood. Neighbors, friends and relatives had been coming and going for days, some having traveled some distance. These oversized drums that resembled large, colorful vases covered with animal skins, accompanied the singer as the African celebration which had gone on for several days came to a celebratory conclusion. Our home for days had been filled with the scent of all varieties of food. Steeped in local tradition, all had come over the previous few days to celebrate the life ahead for the young couple. With a decided lack of entertainment opportunities, everyone looked forward to weddings which became even more important to community life.

The length of the celebration would depend on the overall status and wealth of the family ranging from weeks to days to a one-day event. Ours was decidedly middle class, lasting several days. A large cloth tent was brought in and stretched over the house covering much of the yard. Tables and chairs were set under the tent as well as a stage which provided a spot for the musicians and singer as well as the bride and groom. In many ways, it was very similar to weddings in every part of the world and just went on for a longer period of time – days instead of hours. All who attended contributed towards the cost of the large event and many brought food, decorations and other appropriate gifts to guarantee the success of the celebration.

Unfortunately, in retrospect, I was definitely too young and did not realize just how big a deal marriage was – and the responsibilities a family would bring. But, I was now married, and as far as everyone was concerned, we were ready to begin our life together and were going to visit Egypt to assist my brother during an upcoming surgery, but that's another story.

When you don't get a chance to experience everyday life with someone, it is hard to see their true colors. You only see what they allow you to see. It is basically, like visiting someone's house with advance notice. They have a chance to clean up and tidy the place before your visit and have everything looking perfect for your time spent at their house. Were you to spend a few days, you would get to see many things that you missed in your short, prepared visit. You would have a much more realistic look at life in that home. That's how I felt as soon as we got married. Our wedding was a joint effort from friends and family who basically divided the responsibilities among themselves. Some took care of getting a singer, and some took care of everything in between from the food to the smallest details. Because of them, we had a great gathering of friends where we had all our loved ones by our side. I truly don't remember how I felt at that time. I think it was more of an "expected task" rather than an exciting event.

Chapter 12

A Difficult Road - Flight to Egypt
A long and difficult Journey, and a huge surprise

To properly discuss this, we must back up just a bit, back up to just a short time before our wedding. As our commitment to each other was well known, a wedding was becoming an assumed 'soon to happen event' among our friends and family. BUT, I was becoming quite nervous; I was fearful for what my future might bring. Friends and family were passing on 'whispers' – a comment here, a warning there, from some with contacts within the Khartoum government of al Bashir – all adding up to one inevitable conclusion: the government was tired of having to deal with a pain in their ass young lady named Hagir Elsheikh. I was a candidate for another visit to a Ghost House – perhaps a very FINAL visit. It was made clear to me that leaving Sudan would be a VERY wise move, indeed.

We were sitting together one evening and I took his hand, "Chimera, you've heard the same rumors I have. I think the time has come that we should consider leaving. If we don't get out while we can, I fear that you may join me as a victim to their anger."

"I don't know, Hagir. I'm not so sure that it's that bad. I fear you may be overreacting. This is our home. I want to marry you here and raise our family here. I don't think I'm ready to just leave all our friends and family."

I was frustrated by his hesitancy and indecision. "I'm not ready to have them arrange for me to disappear forever and allow them to win. I don't think there's any choice but to leave and live to fight them another day. We either get out now and survive or stay, get married and risk that marriage being a VERY short one with either me or worse, both of us disappearing."

After much back and forth arguing, I made it very clear my decision was made, that I was leaving – with or without him. I found myself questioning the strength of our love and almost hoping that he would refuse to leave... that he would set me free of my commitment, and I would escape alone to find a new and safer destiny.

Finally, he was simply not ready to give up on our relationship and agreed to leave with me as long as we got married first. We quickly put together a plan which basically worked around my brother Haidar's planned back surgery in Egypt. It required a quickly planned wedding to be followed by a trip to Cairo to assist Haidar during his recovery which would double as a honeymoon.

We went to father for his approval. He knew full well the dangers of staying and agreed that using both Haidar's surgery and the honeymoon as an excuse would be a believable "cover story" for our departure from Sudan. It would be much safer. Traveling with my husband would be far less scrutinized than an unmarried, young girl either traveling alone or even with family – but without a husband. Such was the Islamic male dominance and superiority tradition that the marriage actually made my escape MUCH safer. There was definitely something ironic there. Father also felt that after my mother and Haidar returned home, it would be much safer remaining in Cairo with a husband.

So with father's blessings, we moved ahead with the wedding and our secret departure plan which remained just that – secret from all except a select few. Actually, the short space of time to prepare for our wedding meant many of our friends who were kept in the dark as to our plans were so preoccupied doing their share to help us get ready for the 'big day' that our escape plan was even more likely to work.

***

Unfortunately, I can't describe all we had to go through to escape Sudan. I can't risk the current powers that be reading exactly what their weaknesses are in their systems and how we were able to escape to Egypt before they had any idea that we were gone. I will say that it was a bold and dangerous plan which managed to bypass government regulations and ended with us simply ... Well? Let's just say we got out through sheer nerve and audacity. Suffice to say, we left Sudan to go to Egypt with my mom, my brother Haidar and my sister Nagla tagging along. My brother Diaa was already in Egypt, awaiting our arrival. Haidar of course, was the excuse to go due to assisting him following his scheduled surgery.

As soon as we arrived in Egypt, my husband and I declared our refugee status and began our long and difficult journey to freedom. I was busy either volunteering at a women's organization for kids with mental disabilities, preoccupied with our immigration case and all that had to be done, or had our apartment full of friends. For my "volunteer" work helping give women proper training in this field, I was paid $20 a week which gave us enough food and drink for a couple days each week. Because of all this, I wasn't able to spend much true alone time with my new husband. At the beginning of our difficult stay in Egypt, he only gave quick snapshots of what was to come.

And then, the big surprise! – Totally unexpected, I discovered I was now pregnant. So, I would now have a husband who was growing more distant and even beginning to drink in excess, a baby on the way and after my family left when Haidar had recovered enough to return home, we would be alone as refugees in a dangerous land and with a complex bureaucracy to weave our way through to find our way to safety and freedom. Cairo – though perhaps safer for me than Khartoum – was anything but a safe refuge for a newlywed couple from Sudan... now soon to be a family of three. It was critical that we soon receive refuge in a safer place – hopefully, The United States.

As we continued our lives as refugees and worked through the system in Cairo, the warning signs were there. I started to see 'glimpses' of Chimera's other personalities, but again, I was too overwhelmed by our circumstances to fully understand the warning signs they represented. When we had to collaborate as a team wherever we would be allowed to relocate to and take care of a home and a child together, the true Chimera would rise from the mythological volcano. Much more on that later, but at this time in Egypt, it would be unfair to say that all my time in this relationship was miserable. We had good times and bad times just like any other couple, but my 'bad'... was much worse than a normal bad time. 'Bad' was no longer an accurate description when someone violates your safety and makes your existence unbearable – especially for a pregnant, young woman who now had to worry about the life of her unborn child in addition to her own life.

Chapter 13

Refugee Status – Survival

Leaving Sudan for Egypt stirred many feelings that I wasn't familiar with. I was making so many life decisions in such a short time: from making the decision to leave my homeland, to marrying and becoming pregnant right after, to applying for refugee status. In Egypt, I submitted my case to the UN and became a refugee awaiting my fate. My sister Nagat had already relocated to Philadelphia. With this as an important part of our application and her working for us in the United States, there was hope that we would be accepted there, but there were no guarantees – neither where nor how long it would take were anything we could control. During this time, we had to rely on our own resources to survive. The first few months we were fine, since my family members were with us for Haidar's surgery. He was in severe pain due to back issues and had his surgery scheduled in Egypt. He arranged with one of his lawyer friends for us to stay in his upscale apartment. We had plenty of help from Rashid and some money we managed to save from a fundraising party we had for Haidar in Sudan.

Our stay at that apartment was a good transition for me since we had my mom with us for the first three months in Egypt. It helped me to have her with me in a new place, even for a short period. After the surgery, they all returned to Sudan and left us waiting to be resettled somewhere by the UN. After they left, we had to vacate the apartment and move somewhere we could afford. At this point, things became difficult. I was very depressed during my pregnancy; my hormones were playing games with me. It felt very dark and cold around me. My future was gloomy. I didn't know if my UN case would be accepted and if we would be approved for resettlement or not. I didn't know how we were going to survive the next few months and how we were going to eat, let alone feed a baby that was growing in my body. I wasn't sure about anything else in my life at that time; my whole life had become full of uncertainty. This is what depression is... a real issue that many people refuse to discuss or feel ashamed to admit it. I was at the point where I thought about taking my own life many times. Our first apartment with my family was in a skyscraper, I believe it was in the 12th or the 18th floor; I don't quite remember. What I do remember is that I opened the window many times and looked down. People appeared very small from where I stood. I thought about jumping and ending it all. I don't know what stopped me; perhaps what stopped me was the thought of not hurting my unborn child or just maybe it was everything that I went through and survived over the years... or maybe it was something else. But it was so real, the thoughts and the sadness. I tried to redirect my focus, and I kept myself busy in an attempt to pass the time.

I didn't have anyone to talk to, and every day that passed, I felt a growing distance between me and Chimera. When we began dating back in Sudan, he drank at parties, but I never really saw him drunk. Now, despite our limited resources, he was drinking again. Alcohol is available in Egypt – unlike some of the more conservative Arab countries. This made the growing space between us even wider. It also added to my depression and desperation.

As a couple, we were poor, barely scraping by. Our income was limited to what my siblings were able to send us. My older brother Rashid, who lived in England and my sister, Nagat, who resided in the United States, never failed to send us money every month. Their kindness kept us up-to-date on our rent and provided us with several-days-worth of food.

We had no choice but to wait things out and hope we could survive long enough to finally receive the travel orders to a future home. The procedure was long and drawn out. We applied to the United Nations who vetted us and endorsed our refugee status. Then, our names were given to a couple of non-profit refugee agencies: IOM International Organization for Migration and CWS Church World Services. Both worked with the UN to find an appropriate relocation and also to pass along "survival" funds through their representatives in Egypt to keep us going until they could accomplish their task. Unfortunately, the system set up with locals by both the UN and these agencies is very corrupt. These survival stipends rarely make it to the refugees in such desperate need. The local representatives are so powerful that anyone who knew that had survival money coming was terrified to complain. We simply had no idea who was corrupt and who wasn't. For that matter, we had no idea how far up the corruption went in the organizations and feared that we would be dropped from the wait list completely. Can you imagine how many million refugees are left with no money, no food and no healthcare while their monthly living stipends promised to them were pocketed by supposed aid workers of one of the organizations? Some of these refugees don't even know that they are entitled to some survival money once they are on the list. Often, the corrupt local representatives were the ones who should have notified them. What they don't know about – they won't look for. The entire refugee system in that area is a complete mess and a humanitarian nightmare. Prior to our successful approval to come to the United States, we received not a dollar of the stipend we were told we would receive. We barely survived the system.

I'll always remember how violated I felt that some agency representative jerk was pocketing money that was supposed to guarantee my survival – and my baby's survival, but refugees in Egypt face other dangers – it is a VERY corrupt country. The multitude of refugees already on someone's "official list" awaiting salvation became victims – again – as they were often assaulted and had their live organs harvested by corrupt doctors. These were some of the most desperate people in the world, escaping indescribable war and torture. Most were from either the poor Darfur region of Sudan or from war-ravaged South Sudan. There was often religious persecution involved as many of these refugees were NOT Sunni Muslims as were over 90% of Egypt.

The refugees had to use Egypt as a pass-through to survival somewhere else only to find themselves at the mercy of sick bastards who would steal what little they had and worse still, submit them to atrocities like organ theft. I felt suffocated in that place even before I learned the depth of the corruption. I knew I was escaping to a place that was harsh and dangerous; I just didn't know how harsh and how dangerous. It is not a place friendly to desperate but good intentioned people. You have to be bad and evil yourself, just to survive each day – awaiting your name appearing on one of the UN lists.

This situation should make people think twice about the refugee situation and realize that no one leaves their home unless their home is so dangerous and such a bad situation that the "unknown" becomes a better alternative. Unless desperate, no one would choose to start from point zero in an unknown place where everything is foreign to them: the language, the streets, the way of life unless that home alternative is HELL! They do not choose to put themselves and often their loved ones in such risky situations unless their choice of those dangers is perceived to be safer than staying the course at home – in sickness, starvation and war.

A tiny apartment was all we could afford during our time in Egypt with the money we received from my family. It was located in a bad area in the middle of a complex with steep, spiral steps leading to a one-bedroom studio with a bed separated from the rest of the space by a curtain. The small kitchen contained a stove and a small refrigerator, and you had to watch your calories or you might not fit in the tiny space to cook. A loveseat positioned beside the stove was what we considered our sitting area. Attached to the kitchen was another space with a toilet that served as our bathroom. It was impossible to even stretch out in that small apartment that we called home, but it was the only place our money could get us. This apartment wasn't only small, but it was in an inconvenient location; it was a two-hour train from the city center. The places I needed to be on a regular basis for my job with the women's organization or to follow up on our case were even more distant. When I was short on money, I'd take public transportation as far as my finances would allow, then walk miles further to reach my destination. We had to use our money judiciously and weigh the consequences of walking today and saving for tomorrow or spending today and not eating tomorrow. Many times I fainted on the train from exhaustion, the hot weather combined with the pregnancy or from hunger. I was literally starving to death.

Meanwhile, I was paid the $20 a week for "volunteer" work at the women's organization. The money I earned there, paid for some of my transportation, bread, black tea, and sugar – which we survived on most days. Unfortunately, all too often this small amount of money fell far short – there were far too many days when we had NOTHING… Indeed, I was a starving, pregnant woman. On the rarest of days, we were fortunate enough to buy beans or even the occasional chicken, but that was seldom and a luxury considering our current lifestyle. Our friends often stayed with us in this tiny apartment. I don't know how we all fit in there but we did. Many of them lacked resources and money, and we relied on each other to survive.

When I was in that small studio apartment, lying down after a long day of both walking extreme distances and riding in old smelly trains, I often thought of my life back in Sudan and compared it to what I was going through in Egypt as a refugee with its slim hope for the future and what it might bring. I came to the conclusion that indeed, I might live and I might die. I was probably a 50/50 chance of it going either way. But, had I stayed in Khartoum, Sudan – death was a given. Playing this game of Russian roulette for both myself and my baby was a better option than the alternative. This was true even as we survived barely in that half-studio apartment, in a very bad and dangerous neighborhood. I felt safer there than I was at home. Even with its old bed, ripped, stained raggedy mattress where I often got bit by something – who knows what – I still slept well. Despite the 'oh so worn mattress' which allowed you to feel every lump and every piece of metal sticking through the mattress into your body – I still slept well. Despite the covers so old and threadbare that they hardly provided warmth and comfort – I still slept well. Despite the bites, the dangers, the hunger, each day I awoke I felt one day closer to my destination – my survival and that of my baby.

As for Greater Cairo, the people on the street were not that friendly either, and there, just like in Sudan we faced harassment, overcrowded public transportation (buses, trains etc) and you always feel suffocated. In public you are always put in a situation where strangers are too close, touching you with various parts of their bodies and having people simply act as if nothing happened. The smell of the locals is very distinct: sweat and bad aroma – not a pleasant experience. Refugees including us, travel periodically to the IOM office and check each new list of names for the next plane to salvation in the hope that our name appears – that our final destination is approved and within reach. Just like that in quick glimpse of a list posted on a non-descript wall, your hopes are either restored that life will go on or destroyed in just a few moments as you fail to find your name. When someone who you've befriended appears on the list, we would all celebrate and congratulate them – partially to hide our own disappointment that our turn had not yet come.

Chapter 14

The List – A Woman's Song of Hope

I can't explain the relief and excitement when, finally, I saw my name on the list – giving me the day and flight number to report to fly to the United States. I felt reborn! I couldn't stop smiling, crying and laughing all at once. It wasn't necessary to rush home to pack. You see my entire world boiled down to two or three pieces of clothing, a pair of jeans, two shirts and one dress that had been given to me by my friend, Hala. Oh and I had one old, worn pair of shoes and a bag of books and cassette tapes that had survived this long. That and the wonderful child still in my womb were all I brought to America – that and a renewed hope that I would survive and my baby would flourish.

During this challenging time, some of my friends would often come through for me, bringing me things like vitamins, apples, and greens. That period was difficult both physically and financially, but their visits were often happy times and memories. The many visitors took my mind off my troubles with their readiness to engage in a laugh, or play cards, or just "be" with us.

We were blessed with good friends, and we thought of them as family. One particular friend who is dear to my heart was Mirghani Hamza. The two of us often played cards together to kill time. My eyes get misty when I remember his eyes – so deep, clear and kind. It's as if they were capable of entering your soul and filling you with joy.

Without thinking, Mirghani would drink all the milk in the house at night and then wake up in the morning with regrets realizing I needed it during my pregnancy. I didn't realize that this small mishap stayed on his conscious until years later, long after we left Egypt for the United States. He had said goodbye to me in Cairo and would soon be leaving Egypt to begin a life in Canada. After we said our goodbyes in Egypt, we sometimes chatted on the phone, and after three years, we made a promise to meet at my brother Husham's wedding in Toronto. Mirghani said he was excited to finally meet Malaz, my daughter, and apologize to her for making me anemic during my pregnancy because he drank all the milk. We laughed together and enjoyed a nostalgic walk down memory lane, and I had the opportunity to ease the conscience of this wonderful man and assure him that my daughter was born healthy – despite his forages into my skimpy milk supply.

Much to my shock, just a few days prior to our carefully planned trip to Canada to attend the wedding and catch up with Mirghani, everything changed. I remember walking in from my class at HACC (our community college in Harrisburg), and as soon as I opened the door, I knew something was wrong. Two of our friends were sitting in the living room, along with Chimera. Their faces had that look that told me it was something serious. I felt my knees giving way and a knot forming in my stomach, as I began demanding information as to what had happened. They asked me to sit down and then, informed me that Mirghani died in a car accident. At that moment, I felt the ground lift from under my feet. I was dumbstruck, unable to speak or think. A flood of tears fell from my eyes, as I mourned and tried to understand how this could be possible. We had plans to see each other in the next couple of days. This couldn't be real life. I was in denial for a long time after learning the news, and I have to admit that I was angry at life, angry at him, not to mention all the cars in the world and their drivers, as well. It was an irrational anger, but it was my way of coping I suppose.

I made the decision to travel to Canada for the wedding, but in the end, I couldn't attend. My heart was hurting too much for me to even make an attempt to enjoy the gathering. All I wanted was to be left alone, not surrounded by people. I did make a feeble attempt to attend, but my tears wouldn't let up. I didn't want to dampen the mood for everyone at my brother's wedding, and I knew that he deserved to be happy on his big day. I, however, just couldn't put up a front and pretend that I was ok, so I sat in the parking lot just thinking and crying. In fact, I cried the entire way to Canada, with tears that felt equivalent to that of the Niagara Falls. I grieved my friend for a long time afterwards, and that's when I began pouring words out on paper. I realized that I have many close friends whom I have stories and histories with; some of them were even closer to me than Mirghani, but I also became aware that I might be grieving not just for him, but also for me and my life – my past, the fond memories left behind. Losing someone is tough; it gives you different kinds of feelings towards life – especially when you share a common bond. He became that reality check I needed to wake up I guess. Our memory can be selective sometimes.

The tragic loss of this wonderful man, whose guilt over sharing the milk of his pregnant friend was never absolved... had a tremendous effect on me – one I will never forget – nor do I want to forget this kind and gentle man. We had both survived hard times and challenges in Sudan and as refugees. The challenges of being a refugee searching for work in a country that has a shortage of jobs for its own citizens cannot be understated. Not knowing where and when the next meal will come from is just one of the many worries that stalked us in our day-to-day existence, and yet, we shared with friends what we could while we awaited placement.

The difficult times continued until we were granted entry to the US as refugees and offered a resettlement status and placed on a waiting list. For some, that waiting list is long; it all depends on the circumstances. We were among the lucky ones, and before long, our travel plans were finalized. My baby would be born in the United

States. As I told you earlier, during our stay in Egypt, we were supposed to receive financial assistance from the refugee relief organizations. It never came. I barely survived by will alone and the generosity of my family, and by that time, I was just so tired of fighting and running to get 'here and there' that I just wanted everything to be over – to reach my final destination and settle in my new home and have my baby. From the torture tree at the Ghost House, to having to sneak into the university just to attend classes, to having a bounty on my head and fleeing my homeland, to allowing my baby to survive – I continued my desperate journey. With each successive step, I came closer to my goal. I came closer to *Climbing On The Clouds.*

Chapter 15

Hope for a New Beginning - Relocation to America

But I get ahead of myself. It's important to understand my journey from Sudanese Refugee status in Egypt, to freedom in – appropriately – the home of America's Liberty Bell, Philadelphia, Pennsylvania in the United States of America.

When it was time to leave Egypt behind, I was bursting with hope for a new life and a bright future as I boarded a plane with nothing but a bag full of books and some clothes. I found the twelve hour flight to be quite miserable because I was VERY pregnant. I tried walking, but nothing helped as my feet started to swell larger and larger. It didn't help that the flight was overfilled with people from different countries, and the sounds and smells were overwhelming in my delicate condition. The baby seemed to be reaching up my throat and grabbing at whatever… as time ticked away slowly. It seemed as if every minute was an hour.

When we finally reached our destination in Philadelphia, my sister Nagat, my brother-in-law and one of their friends greeted us warmly, and soon, we were on our way to our final destination. I remember looking outside and seeing what looked like slums and wondering if the plane took a wrong turn back to Egypt. I was so tired at this time that I couldn't wait to make it back to my sister's house to finally get some sleep. I fell asleep right away and when I woke up the next day, I felt refreshed but still uncertain as to what would come next. Because my sister and brother-in-law were acting as our financial sponsors, they agreed to keep us in their home and take care of us to facilitate placement. We arranged to meet with a representative who advised us on getting our legal papers together while helping us with medical assistance and job searches.

I received immediate medical care as I entered the States due to my pregnancy. Unfortunately, things took a bad turn when my sister, Nagat, fell down and broke her ankle while hanging curtains. The injury left her with a cast, and she was bedridden for a short time. I, too, was bedridden for three weeks, due to my condition. This was another challenge that we had to overcome, yet, we managed to make it work with some difficulty.

Finally, the day arrived when I was to give birth. On August 16, after twelve hours of labor, Malaz entered the world both healthy and beautiful. I remember each moment of that day with great detail. My water broke while I was at home, but I hadn't realized it. I started having pains and the constant urge to go to the bathroom. Finally, my sister told me to call the doctor and describe my situation. Soon enough, they told me to head to the hospital. It was almost 1:40 a.m. when we arrived at the hospital, and they took me back straight away. I immediately asked for anesthesia to stop the pain. It was excruciating and I felt like I was going to die. The moment I saw her face all of the pain disappeared. We only had to stay at the hospital for twenty-four hours before they sent us home. When we got home, everyone left me and my sister alone including Chimera. They said they were going to celebrate at a friend's house which translated to "going drinking". A while after they left, I started to get hungry. I was so famished that when I attempted to get up to go to the kitchen, I fainted and fell to the floor. When I realized what happened, the struggle hit me all at once, and all I could do was sit there on the floor and sob. I think that was the first time that I really missed my home country of Sudan, my mother, father, other siblings and my friends. I felt alone and weak, with an aching longing for everyone and everything that I left behind.

After about a month and a half, Chimera and I visited our friends Waleed and his wife in Harrisburg, and I really liked the "quietness" of the area – at least compared to the hustle and bustle of Philadelphia. They were kind enough to take us in and helped me find work at a nearby daycare. I felt it was a good move at the time. Not only would I earn an income, but I would also be able to spend time with my daughter while learning about the culture and brushing up on the language. What a huge step this was for me – just four months after arriving in the United States and six weeks after giving birth, I was working at a job. That ended up being a huge turning point in my life.

Before long, we were able to be self-sufficient and rented our first apartment in the city. Because it was far from my job and I couldn't afford a car at that time, I relied on public transportation, carrying my daughter along with me. It was especially hard during the winter time. It was my first winter in the US, and the weather in Harrisburg was rough. Not only did I slip often, but many times I couldn't feel my hands or face. It took me back to my childhood. Back to the days where I would walk to school in the freezing wind wondering how my body could fight against such treacherous weather. The culture was foreign and the weather conditions were challenging, but I'd been through too much to allow that to defeat me. I constantly reminded myself that I was strong. My body was strong and my mind was strong. I wouldn't be defeated easily.

With the help from my friend Waleed and my other friend Osman, I learned how to drive. I remember when I attempted to take the driver's test the first time. I was so nervous and anxious to get my license that I put the car in reverse before turning it on, which caused me to fail before I even realized it. Unaware of my mistake, I tried to start the car... nothing happened. The examiner looked at me and asked why I thought the car wouldn't turn on. Looking at him confused, I told him I didn't know. He asked me to think about it, but by the time I realized the silly mistake, I knew I had blown my chance. So overwhelmed, I didn't know if I should laugh or cry at that moment. It was a great lesson because I taught myself that I needed to be patient, and sometimes, it is better to spend an extra minute to think rather than jumping into something and making a mistake that could set me back. I had to reschedule for the next available spot they had to retake the test. Pretty soon, I acquired my license and a used car. It wasn't great, but it was mine, and I was finally able to get a break from public transportation and set my sights on even higher goals.

Prior to purchasing my car, I decided to register at our community college, HACC (Harrisburg Area Community College), and with my friend Osman's help, I began taking classes in the evenings after work. He lent me his car and helped me get to and from classes. Since I had a degree from a University in Sudan, I wasn't sure if I wanted to continue the Engineering path or choose a different career. Osman helped by introducing me to a counselor and got me on the right track. I was able to do a placement test to assess my level. I was placed at a college level in English and math. Since I wasn't sure what my major would be, I started by taking general academic classes. I was also looking for flexibility, since I had to continue working at the daycare full time. I would start working at 7 a.m. and worked until 5:30 p.m. After work, I dropped Malaz off at one of the neighbors who babysat her until I returned to get her at 10:30 p.m. I did this day in and day out, because I knew that with an education I could give us a better life. I consider myself one of the lucky ones who was able to overcome a series of struggles, but I am not going to lie and say my journey was easy.

HACC remains after all these years as a wonderful institution that made this life-giving education possible. Truly they made it easy for me – and others like me – to get a college degree. The teachers were understanding and helpful. I can't imagine a better place at the time to assist me in hitting the ground running. This is especially true when you remember that although my English was reasonably good, it was still my second language, and this fact sometimes caused educational difficulties.

The curriculum was flexible. I was able to take additional online courses which allowed me to raise children, work to survive financially and eventually, receive my associate degree in Nursing. It was both the institution of... and the people at Harrisburg Area Community College who made it possible for me to succeed and achieve the education necessary – an education which became the foundation of my success. I was able to continue my education and received my bachelor degree. It was during this time that HACC gave me an opportunity to work as a Clinical Instructor, teaching nursing students at their Lancaster Campus. Education allowed me to start my own business, HSE Staffing Agency. I was now getting a much better grip on my life.

I realize now, that it was my own perseverance and determination to achieve a stable college education along with the help, understanding and assistance of everyone working at HACC that allowed me to survive, establish a successful business, raise my children and continue to advocate for a better world by communicating some of the awful things I have had the misfortune to witness throughout my relatively short but eventful life to this point.

My strengths academically and in business were recently recognized by my alma mater when I was appointed to the HACC Board of Trustees, the overseers charged with guiding the campus community, administrators – students – staff, down the path of success. I spoke recently at one of their graduation ceremonies and got to pass their diplomas to "my" students. As I accomplished this, I couldn't help but think back on my college experience in Sudan and how difficult it was to accomplish anything due to the corruption involved and the prejudice which dominates that society – prejudice toward women. My being female was the first major roadblock placed before me. In these African societies, there are no opportunities to grow as a woman... there is no support to your dreams of a successful future, one that could be accomplished through education. While I watched my smiling students – safe in Pennsylvania with their dreams of success and a future equal to those dreams – walk across the stage, my mind thought of all the young female dreamers in Sudan who have so much to offer their society, but only because they possess the wonderful ability to give new life and a few more curves to their bodies than their male counterparts, those dreams deteriorate to song: *'To Dream The Impossible Dream'*. (With apologies and credit to Don Quixote and *'The Man From La Mancha'*)

As I watched these wonderful students in their caps and gowns signifying this next level of achieved educational experience, I remembered my first college experience and remembered how much of a constant hustle, constant struggle my college experience in Sudan had been. I remembered how just being a woman trying to get an education was in itself, enough to single me out as someone to be scorned and – indeed – feared, as I represented the basic insecurities of their male-dominated society that simply couldn't accept that a lowly female – a creature created to accept their sexual advances and provide them with heirs as well as accomplish their household burdens – was capable of having a desire to learn and advance herself while successfully understanding something as complicated as Electrical Engineering and even achieving a degree most of them would be incapable of.

And then, I – again – looked at our HACC students receiving their degrees and thought of how lucky they are that their freedoms and systems allow them to easily attend college. If necessary, you can work and still attend college and even graduate. Their flexible schedules and classes make it easier for a mother especially to fulfill her dreams and yet, still be able to care for her children if she has to.

A single mother in Sudan can only achieve a shameful status. They are automatically recognized as someone at fault for their own circumstance – guilty of an unforgivable sin against society. They receive no help from their country. They receive no help from their community. They receive no help from their families. They have no ability to become "something" and are treated pretty much as if they are dead. And heaven forbid if you have kids and have for whatever justifiable reason become divorced… again, you might as well die, and the children of these single parents are born into a life that forever will bear the stigma of the mother's shame and guilt. Laws favor the men – allowing them to block the mother from taking any children out of the country and making it easy for the male to sue for custody and avoid any financial obligations toward the wife or children. Women will very likely lose any custody battle no matter what their justifiable grounds might be.

Were I to have gone through what I have gone through in Sudan instead of the United States, I can't even imagine what would have happened. It is safe to assume I would not have survived – let alone have two wonderful, beautiful daughters, a wonderful husband and a successful business. All of those thoughts crossed my mind during that brief time on the stage at graduation, and I was filled with pride and recognized just how privileged I am to have been accepted by this society, by this community, and by all these wonderful new friends here at HACC. I will never take my life and circumstances for granted, and I will certainly never take everything I went through to get to this point in my life for granted either. This is why I continue to do everything I can to help others and continue a life that not only I can be proud to have lived but my daughters will also appreciate and emulate and work towards joining their mother in making life a bit better, a bit easier for all their fellow citizens of this big blue planet we call earth.

It may sound corny, but truly... anything can be successfully accomplished if you just put your mind to it. I quite literally had an entire government in my way, an entire army and security force in my way – trying to stop me at every intersection. However, because I was so determined to have a better life for myself and my family, I was able to achieve it. I was able to survive and flourish. I was able to *Climb On The Clouds*.

Chapter 16

In My Father's Footsteps – Again

During this time at the daycare, I learned about a two-week course that will qualify me to become a Certified Nurse's Aide (CNA). The only problem was that I had to come up with the money for the class. It was $500 that needed to be paid in advance, and I just couldn't afford that. Thinking of ways that I could pay for the program, I decided to apply for a credit card at my bank. To my surprise, I got approved and the biggest wave of relief came over me. I registered for the class, and I was assigned a date to start. Choosing to start at HACC and to start with this program was a life-changing decision for me.

Looking back at my decision, I am so proud of myself for believing that I could do it. Who would have ever thought that assisting father with injections, administering medications and starting IV's with people so desperate for medical help that they would welcome assistance from one so young... would lead to a new life – with new friends – in a new country?

Once I started in the class, it was actually quite easy for me, minus the part where I had to change an adult diaper. Even though I knew this was a noble job, I was nauseated, sick to my stomach, but I had no other choice but to pull through and try to normalize it. I remember I wasn't able to eat or drink the whole day. Soon enough, I got used to the smell, and I started looking at it differently. I enjoyed my job as a CNA. I was able to help people, talk to them, and feel like I was making a difference. Even though this certificate was only a small step, I was proud to tell people I had it. In a sense, it made me feel connected to my father. I now understood the satisfaction he must've felt helping the people of our village so long ago. The other positive thing about this job was its security, because it was such a high demand field. This was so important because our income was reduced to one, mine.

I'm quite sure at this point that you must be wondering... where is my husband during all this. For a time, he did have a job, but he continued to drink, and since he had taken a job as a taxi driver, well??? Let's just say a job as a professional driver and being a heavy drinker do not go well together. Chimera had lost his job due to a DUI, and to keep our finances afloat, I was forced to work at the hospital at night from 11 p.m. to 7 a.m., come home and take Malaz to my job at the daycare where I would use the bathroom to get ready to begin work again from 8 a.m. to 5 p.m. You may wonder when I managed to get any sleep – my lunch hour became my nap hour. I managed to rest for a few hours after I returned from the daycare and before going in for my night shift at the hospital. Working as a CNA was very hard. Many times, we had to manually lift heavy patients, and you are basically on your feet the whole time. The routine was tough. Starting with an early morning bath or shower to your assigned patients, then getting them dressed and out of bed for breakfast. After you finish feeding them, you have to take them to the bathroom, change their brief if they are incontinent and then, take them to their activities. Before you know it, it is time for their nap, then toileting them again, getting them out of the bed one by one and taking them for lunch. Then, do it all over again after lunch, and if you are staying for 16 hours, then the same routine continues from seven in the morning to eleven at night, which I did often. This madness continued on for three months, during which time I was exhausted beyond imagination, but I felt like I had no other choice but to continue.

Eventually, I was accepted into the nursing clinical program. Things were starting to look up. I was making more money and on the right track for the field that I chose. With a heavy heart and fear from the unknown future, I had to say goodbye to my first job at the daycare. I had to move on in order for me to grow. I am thankful to everyone there and for the experience and strength I got from being around the Daycare family who had become one of my early support groups – critical to my future successes.

Chapter 17

A Victim of a Different Kind – Surviving Domestic Abuse

To properly discuss this significant part of my life, we must back up a bit. Prior to leaving the daycare, I had a tough time not only with my school and work life but even with my personal life. My now ex-husband was drinking heavily every day which affected us financially and emotionally. He became a different person when he was drunk. He didn't have any plans for the future nor did he care about anything but enjoying the moment. Because he didn't work enough to even secure the "taxi rental fee" for his job, he often used my hard-earned income without my permission to either pay his taxi rent or to support his other habits. When it came to my finances, I was too busy with work, school and my baby to keep track of my income and my expenses as closely as I should have and failed to watch my credit card which he was using without my permission, and I also didn't expect this to happen:

On the weekend, when the taxi drivers are working and making a large part of their income, he often stayed at the nightclubs, was drinking at his friends' houses or had his friends over to our house drinking. He became violent and often raised his voice at me. It soon deteriorated further and he progressed to physical abuse.

When my ex-husband first put his hands on me, our friend Waleed was there to witness the incident. I was shocked and bruised both mentally and physically. My clothes were ripped and a range of emotions overtook me. Like many domestic abuse victims, I felt humiliation, hurt, surprise, and I was full of fear. Our friend Waleed intervened while I grabbed Malaz and ran to the car and locked us both inside. He followed us and started banging on the door; after all I had been through, I never thought I could be afraid of someone… so close to me as I did that night. After so many years as a victim of my government in Sudan, the man I thought I loved, the man who was the father of my daughter made me a victim once again – a victim of another kind – spousal abuse. I was a battered woman.

Waleed followed him out to our car and forced him back into our home while Malaz and I stayed in the car until he had fallen asleep – more likely, passed out. Later, Waleed came out and informed me that it was safe to come inside. When I felt relatively secure, I ran inside and packed a bag for me and my daughter, then locked my room to sleep for a few hours before deciding what to do next. The next morning, I drove to the daycare. I can recall every detail. It was a Thursday and I needed the money from my Friday paycheck as well as a place to stay. After calling my sister, she wanted to come and get me, but I told her I would drive to their house after I got my check at work. I didn't tell anyone where I would be, in fear that my Chimera would go searching for me. My co-workers and boss saw the painful black-and-blue bruises on my face and shoulder and advised me to file a "protection from abuse" order, but I was hesitant. I came from a different culture: a culture where it is shameful to speak about violence, and in some parts, it is not only normal – it's expected. It is also unacceptable to call the police or seek help. You would be considered a bad wife or a "bad woman" so to speak. All that came to my mind while I was listening to my coworkers, and I just ended up calling my sister and decided to go to their house and figure things out there instead.

Not that I agree with many things that we were raised to believe in back in Sudan, both cultural and religion, but when things are hammered into your head for so long, sometimes they resurface and surprise you. Looking back on it, I couldn't believe my thought process at that time. You could say I froze or remained in a denial stage for a long time. Yes, my experience back in Sudan made me a fighter – especially considering everything I previously endured, but this time, I felt that I failed to fight.

I am sure many victims of abuse will relate to my situation. As we all know now, abusers can have many different masks, but sooner or later, all those masks will fall, and you will be able to see their ugly side. You don't believe this is happening to you; you are in shock and refuse to believe you are, indeed, in an abusive relationship.

My boss was kind enough to offer me a temporary sanctuary that night at the daycare center where I worked. After everyone left, we closed the daycare, turned off the light and armed the security system alarm. Malaz and I lay on the kids' mat, ready for a long night. The daycare was located in a rough area where gunshots and break-ins were common. I was so scared that I held my baby close that night and for many nights to come and longed for a day when I could sleep soundly. I didn't sleep a wink that night. How could I when my life was turned upside down? The fear of the unknown and the hurt were beyond my ability to tolerate. Memories of the past mingled with troublesome thoughts about the future... and my head was flooded with uncertainty!

I woke up early that morning before people arrived and brushed my and Malaz's teeth. We couldn't shower that day, since the daycare had no shower facilities. Soon enough, everyone arrived and we started our last workday of the week.

I finished my work day and headed off to my sister's house in Philadelphia where I recounted the entire story and shared my plans for divorce. It shouldn't have come as a surprise when people began to reach for reasons and justify his reprehensible behavior.

"Maybe he's under stress; give him a chance," they said.

"This is the first time he's gotten physical. He was under the influence," and repeated all the excuses that people make... instead of admitting the ugly truth. Not long afterwards, he came to my sister's house, overflowing with promises and apologies… all of which persuaded me to give him another chance. We as a society are too fast to blame the victim, to shame them and make them feel it is their fault – they are the cause of the abuse, the guilty party instead of the victim. This was classic spousal abuse "course 101" – convince the victim that they are the one responsible for the actions of the abuser. They surely must have done something to provoke the actions of their spouse. The "guilt trip" allows the vicious circle of violence to continue.

Should I have known better? Sure, but deep down inside I wanted to believe that the person I married had just made a mistake. I reasoned with myself: he is the father of my child and maybe he just needs help, because in my mind at that time, like many others, I believed the stigma about domestic violence. After all, how could this be domestic violence? I'm a fighter and a strong woman. At this time, I believed the myth that domestic violence only happened to weak individuals who allowed it. Soon enough, I learned from my own experience that this is, of course, just that – a myth. I wanted to believe that I am still the same strong person who grew up fighting an entire government and a system that pitted a diminutive teen-aged girl against entire police and security forces; I wanted to believe that he just made a mistake. I convinced myself that I have always been strong. I had just fallen for a man who seemed to be full of love and ambition – only to be hiding an evil mind behind a sweet face. Regardless of what went on in my mind at the time, I went back, but from that moment, something major was broken in our relationship. Even my attempts to pretend that the abuse didn't happen… didn't work.

During this emotional rollercoaster, I had to drop out from clinicals the second week as life at home became so difficult. I was broken inside and I also had to work extra hours to continue supporting the house. Our relationship became distant. I started losing all respect for this man whom I didn't know anymore. He continued drinking and switching from one job to another. I worked long hours to keep us going financially but also, to keep busy and honestly, to avoid any interaction with him. I applied for the next available clinicals. Once I was accepted into the program and the clinicals started, I was so busy with my daughter, work and school that I didn't have any time for anything else in life – including my spouse.

I asked myself, "How did a fighter for women's rights ever get herself in this predicament?" The irony was piercing. I fled Sudan to avoid violence, only to face it in my own house, delivered at the hands of someone I trusted. The mask had fallen away to reveal his ugly side. Had I been in denial and simply refused to see this side of him? Was I in shock? I just couldn't wrap my mind around the fact that the man I loved could hurt me so deeply. Yet another life lesson… that not everyone is as they seem. Sometimes, when the façade is peeled away, we find something quite different, something quite ugly.

I was sure I was going through the stages of grief. My thoughts were all over the place as I thought about what my future might hold. Where would I live? How would I make it as a single mother? What would others think of me for leaving him? Am I doing the right thing?

At such a difficult time in my life, there were so many individuals who reached out to help me. Whatever I needed, day or night, someone had my back. I truly don't think I would have made it without all of them. I look back and I have to give credit to my boss and coworkers for seeing the signs of domestic abuse and helping me to find my own way out. Who knows how long I could've been trapped in that situation if they hadn't stepped up and asked to be allowed to help me?

**

I kept working very hard in an effort to improve living conditions for us and finally, found myself in a position to purchase a house. I applied for a mortgage, and with the help of my friend Waleed, I bought my first house. Then, one day while driving home from school, I was hit broadside by a tractor trailer and my car was totaled. The entire driver's side was destroyed. It was one of those rare accidents where it was a freak thing – I was thrown by the force of the impact into the passenger seat away from most of the destruction. Surprisingly, I only had minor injuries. The driver's seat area was totally destroyed; I was fortunate to have survived. The accident didn't prevent me from finishing clinicals and graduating on time. Looking back on it, this was a blessing in disguise. During the month I spent at home recuperating; I was able to reflect on my life and what had become of it. I realized I had lost interest in so many things that I used to enjoy and was now in a place where I was accepting things I would never before have allowed. I no longer recognized myself.

A flood of questions flashed across my mind. Who is this person who was once a fighter? This person who would never permit the mistreatment of others? Why do I deserve any less? What do I want for my daughter? Is this why I fought all those years and left my family behind?

Our future disappeared the minute he laid his hands on me, and the rest was basically, a failed attempt to resuscitate a lifeless relationship. I tried my best to make things work even though I knew I was making a mistake. I finally, came to the conclusion that once you lose respect for someone, it is difficult to continue pretending everything is alright. Despite all that happened, I still managed to finish my clinicals and graduate school on time. Near the end of the school year, I had allowed Chimera to take the baby back to Sudan for a visit with the family. I was to follow soon, and after graduation, I flew back to Sudan for the first time since I left and rejoined my daughter. It felt so good seeing everyone again and being able to forget my hectic life back in Harrisburg – safe in the comfort of my family.

My innermost thoughts had not changed. It was my intent to talk to my father about getting his blessings to allow me to end the broken, now abusive relationship with my husband. When I saw how much older and frailer father was, I decided against troubling him further with my problems. While he knew I had to flee Sudan, he was against me moving so far away – halfway around the world, in the first place, and now, confronting him with this and considering his poor health didn't seem like such a good idea. After these second thoughts, I talked to my mother instead. She is against divorce in general and joined with many of my family and friends in Sudan in asking me to reconsider – to give my marriage another chance. The culture and tradition in Sudan are respected more than the law. Despite any physical abuse, it is really hard to get approval from the community and from the extended family when you go against the tradition and culture so firmly embedded in all. In many cases, women's opinions simply don't matter, especially when it comes to major decisions like marriage and divorce. My parents and siblings were open-minded and that at least they allowed me to argue my case with them without any repercussions. Other women in a similar situation might face dire consequences just for discussing divorce. But when it comes to ending a marriage, even my open-minded family could be a little harsh. I know my father would've understood and supported me if I explained it all to him, but that would not prevent him from worrying. In my case and since I was only visiting

116

for a month, I didn't want to upset him and stir things up. His health came before my needs. I decided to drop it and return to the States again to try to make it work.

Malaz was almost five years old and this trip turned out to be a very pleasant experience for her. She was just old enough to have some memories of her only trip to Sudan but more importantly, she got to meet her grandparents and many other family members. She was able to see what life was like there and even play in the streets with some of the other children. Taking lessons from her mother, she LOVED the sand – but we did make sure she didn't follow in my footsteps into the desert in search of her destiny. However, she did spend days playing in the sand and discovered that she could even slide down the sand piles near my father's home. With little water and no showers, she brought a part of Sudan home with her as we were days getting all the sand out of her hair and the nooks and crannies of her body. All in all, allowing her father to bring her to Sudan while I completed my course work and exams ended up being an excellent decision. She has memories and experiences critical to her development.

When we returned, things were calm in the house... for a while at least. He promised to stay on track this time and even applied to a college. He started taking classes and I thought this might actually work out. Maybe I fixed the abuser in him, and maybe we can work this relationship out after all.

During this time, I got pregnant again, and the abuse returned... like a bad dream. Our visit to Sudan became the calm before the storm. Abuse soon became the norm – again. Walking on eggshells became a way of life. Anything and everything could make him lose his temper, and he would start breaking things. This would then escalate into an argument, which turned into physical abuse. Eventually, I avoided conversation with him altogether, choosing instead to work twelve to sixteen hours a day and taking additional online classes. His drinking continued to worsen, and soon, I dreaded even going home at night.

The relationship rollercoaster affected not only my personal life, but it also took a toll on my professional life as well. I was an LPN at this time and taking additional courses toward my RN but had to pick up extra work to continue supporting the family. We, as a couple, became distant from each other. It became clear that I no longer could support a relationship with this "stranger"... whose drinking and job-hopping became progressively worse.

Once again, I questioned myself. As he began missing more work and drinking more, it gradually dawned on me just how huge a mistake I had made. I always tell patients and friends about the abuse cycle and how the abuser is beyond help, but it was me who was guilty of being an enabler. When will I stop? If I continue like this, who knows, the end result might be death.

I understand that domestic violence is a tough issue that takes many forms both physical and emotional. Many women stay due to shame, or because they lack the will or resources to take a stand and leave. Keep in mind that abusers suffer from insecurity, whether it be in romance, jealousy or the fact that a mate may be more successful. Some men just can't handle a strong woman. For them, it's simply a power struggle and a way to assert dominance. Don't allow this to stop you from being your authentic self. Carry your strength and success with pride and never apologize for being who you are. Celebrate that and know that you can make a difference every day. You are limitless; don't allow anyone to convince you otherwise. Refuse to lower your standards for anyone and never accept anything less than what you deserve. I know that now... but back then, it was all a blur.

In my case, the abuse took several forms, from verbal to physical. I was choked and hit with objects while pregnant. I was dragged, left bloody and threatened more times than I can count. Each individual reacts differently. Most victims, myself included, go through many phases, starting with denial and ending with acceptance. Some even buy the abuser's line that it's the victim's fault. This is a common tactic. In my case, I felt that I could help him and perhaps enable him to change. In the end, the key word was "enable", and all I did was hurt myself and delay my new beginning. I eventually, came to the conclusion that enough was enough. It took me more than five years to realize that change for him was but an illusion. That was when I decided to move on. This was not an easy thing to do. Not only was it hard to break out of the cycle, but I would also have to face my family for this decision. We strive for approval from our families and society, but at some point, it's important to realize that little matters when one is in danger of being injured or killed.

When your spouse or partner, or anyone for that matter, chokes you or hits you with objects until you bleed, it's time to run for your life. That's what happened to me. Malaz awoke in the middle of the night to the sounds of him throwing things and choking me. I was almost eight months pregnant, and he was choking me without regards to my condition, blind to the fact that I was carrying a life inside of me, his own flesh and blood. I felt like I was going to die that night and was unable to breathe. At that moment, I realized in my heart that this was the end of the line if I didn't leave. He finally let go of me after I pointed to Malaz and said, "Your daughter is watching you." Then, I ran to my phone and attempted to call two of our friends because I wanted to leave the house. He proceeded to snatch the phone from my hands, breaking it, then blocking my car. When I ran to the house phone, he yanked it from the socket and finally threw my keys at me and demanded that I get out.

I drove my car to a nearby elementary school and sat in the parking lot, turned on the heat and locked my windows until the morning, hoping that he would sober up, so I could return to my daughter. When I finally returned, the apology cycle started. He saw the scratches on my face and the bruises on my neck and body and continued to say that it wouldn't happen again. He was right. It wouldn't happen again because I was leaving, for my safety, my daughter's safety and my unborn child's safety.

I decided that it was really and truly over this time, and there was no turning back. My brother flew in from England to speak with him. He then promised to go to rehab, but it was too late for our marriage, and I knew he wouldn't honor the agreement anyway. Even if he did, I was way past the point of forgiveness, but I agreed to allow him to stay in the basement like a roommate. The pact was that we would continue to raise the kids while he got his act together and attended rehab.

Of course, as soon as my brother left, he refused rehab and hid drinks in the house. I was slapped, kicked, and spit on until finally, I decided to lock him out of the house. He then proceeded to break the balcony glass door with the chairs from the shed. Once again, I called my brother-in-law and we demanded that he leave for good. At that time, I decided I would not allow anyone to stop me from leaving – including my family.

"It is MY life and no one else is forced to live with the daily abuse and the scars that my girls will carry with them if I stay," I told myself. After that, I filed for divorce and changed the locks, closing this chapter... or so I thought.

When presented with the divorce papers, he refused to sign them. My response? "We can do this the easy way or the hard way. It is your choice." I shouldn't have been surprised when harassment ensued. He called my phone every day leaving voicemails and text messages and stalking me by driving past the house. I woke up one night to go to the bathroom, and I saw his car parked on the grass near my front door with the engine running. I mustered up some courage, screamed for him to leave, and threatened to call the police. He left, but the harassment continued. I had no choice but to threaten to file harassment charges against him if he didn't stop. Finally, I decided to use technology against him – it's an amazing invention called "call blocking"

I reflect back on that time in my life with sadness and the painful scars that are left with me when I gaze in the mirror. I take the time to recall the details, but I remain triumphant knowing that my future is now under _my_ control.

One thing that came out of this whole experience was my girls. I wouldn't trade the feeling they give me for anything in the world. Remaz came during this bad time, while I was fighting many battles. She was beautiful and tiny. She came 3 weeks early and had complications during birth which caused her to spend 3 days in the Neonatal Intensive Care Unit (NICU). She weighed 5 pounds, and I felt responsible for her harsh beginning. I blamed myself, like so many survivors of abuse do, for staying with her father. I blamed myself for allowing her to go through much while she was in my womb. I cried every night when she was at the NICU. I hoped to hold her in my arms without tubes and without IV's and wires coming from her body. When she was finally released, I was so relieved. She was still underweight, and I started feeding her formula instead of breast milk to prevent her from working so hard to suck. I didn't want her to be exhausted. During her first year, I was able to continue working and attend school, but it was tough. Having two kids is a lot for a single mother, but I was lucky to have Malaz and some good friends to help me through it all.

Remaz has grown to become a very special girl. Her kind heart and willingness to help others makes everyone around her adore her. It didn't hurt that she was very sweet and beautiful. Her smile can light up any room she is in. As she grew, I noticed she was very talented in music and she has a beautiful voice. I registered her with a piano teacher. Soon enough, she asked to play the violin and join the school band and chorus. She loved acting but was a bit shy in front of others. Her character made it easy for her to make peace with our situation. Malaz and I made sure that she didn't need anything and didn't feel as if she was missing anything. Her memories of her dad were few and close to none, regardless of my attempts to co-parent and put our differences aside when it comes to our responsibilities as parents.

Deep down, my brother Rashid's words stuck in my mind when he once told me that all his attempts to fix my marriage were for the girls. He wanted them to feel the same way we did when we talked about our dad. He wanted them to be proud, to point to him and say that THIS is my father. It was hard for him to understand that you can't wish for a good father and just expect one to show up. Unfortunately, sometimes you have to play the cards life has dealt for you even if they were bad ones. I and all my siblings were very lucky to have such a good father.

Chapter 18

A Goodbye to Elhakeem

I didn't know life could bring more bad news until one day while at work I received a phone call from my sister, Nagla. She told me that my father hadn't been feeling well. They decided to take him to the doctor where they found out that he was in the late stage of pancreatic cancer. The news was a nightmare. I didn't know how to feel. I immediately called my bosses and told them I was traveling for an indefinite amount of time. I gathered what money that I had, bought our plane tickets, packed bags for the girls and left the next day. Remaz was only seven months old at that time. The plane ride was quite a problem since she was so little and cried the whole time. Since we bought our tickets at the last minute, I didn't have many options. We had to accept the first flight out which had a long connection. I didn't think about that because I was preoccupied with my father's health condition. After almost twenty-four hours, we reached our destination and went straight to the hospital.

He was lying in a rusty bed in the middle of a long room with many other beds filled with patients. There were no privacy curtains, fans or even decent equipment. I was so worried about his condition and mad at the poor facilities, all at the same time. I was worried about his well being and mad at the government for not having any regulations or concerns about its people. This wasn't a surprise to me since I knew the Sudanese government was corrupt, but again, I didn't think they could sink to this level. My father was breathing heavily, more like struggling to breathe. I asked my sister how long he had been like that, and she told me the nurses hadn't been taking proper care of him. They didn't check his blood sugar all day until my sister asked them to do so, and by that time, he was basically in a diabetic coma. After a while, we were able to correct it, and he was able to see us and talk. I brought some equipment with me from the US that allowed us to check his blood sugar and blood pressure on our own. We basically lost trust in the hospital, so we decided to start helping the other patients as well. My sister brought a fan that we used for my dad, and I brought some protein shakes and medicine to help his pain. We were all there by his side day in and day out. We had to be, after all, he wasn't an ordinary father, and I couldn't bear the thought of losing him.

Soon after, we were able to move him to a private room. Everything was expensive in Sudan. You have to pay out of pocket and in advance to receive any kind of care, and it wasn't good care to begin with. If you can't afford it, you would simply die. We were in his room all day, and my brothers didn't leave his side at night. They helped him to go to the bathroom and bathed him. It was hard for all of us to see him in pain and unable to care for himself. He was so skinny. It was like death was slowly taking him. He tried to look strong by not showing he had pain, but sometimes, the pain was too intense. Soon, the medication stopped helping him, and he asked us to take him home. He didn't want to stay at the hospital any longer. He just wanted to have us taking care of him at home. We honored his wishes and got an oxygen tank, wheelchair, and other medical equipment to make him comfortable. We took him back to the emergency room a few times after that, but he wasn't happy with that so we kept him home.

It was such a miserable time for him. It continued for almost 3 months, and towards the end, his situation deteriorated and he became unconscious and unable to eat. We put a feeding tube in and continued taking care of him. We gave him different kinds of pain medication including morphine. We continued to talk to him. One night, my mom sat by his head and started talking to him and he responded. I will never forget how he looked at my mom and asked her to take a walk with him by the river and swim. Let me remind you, this is a man who grew up in Sudan – land of deserts – and I don't believe he ever took my mom for a walk by the river, let alone swam with him. Then, he asked her to sing an old kids' song mom used to sing for us to put us to sleep. Mom started singing the song for him and he looked so peaceful. Then, he went back into another coma. It was a short-lived moment for him to be awake, and he continued to open his eyes briefly until one day he took one long breath and stopped. I screamed so hard and started CPR on him. I knew he was gone, but I still tried so hard until my brother Rashid snapped me out of it. Everyone else began to hear the news, and they started the pre-burial process. Doing CPR on my own father was the hardest thing I've ever done, and it will never escape from my mind. This is the second time I witnessed the lost of someone in our house. First was my sister Amal, and now my dad. Of course my parents lost two other children before my time, but this time I was there and I was old enough to understand why everyone was so sad, and I understood why I was crying. We had the burial ritual and the service which included all of the family members who could make it, friends and neighbors. Normally, it lasts three days, and after four days, I left Sudan and came home. When I left, I felt as if I was leaving a part of me. I was leaving my biggest fan and cheerleader, my idol, my best friend and above all, my father. He was someone who made me what I am today and definitely molded me through education into the success I am now. He stood in front of his large family and allowed each of his children to live the lives they deserved as human beings while we watched as he fought for the rights of others. He was someone who led by example and practiced what he preached. While I love my mother dearly, it was clearly my father who is responsible for everything I am today. Every time I fight for the rights of all women, every time I fight against spousal abuse, every time I campaign against female genital mutilation, every time I march in protest to a despot dictator who would hang and beat teenage girls, starve babies and murder innocents at will – I emulate the examples set in stone in my personality by my great father, Seed Ahmed Elsheihk – a true humanitarian who spent his entire life trying to make life better for others.

When I came back to the U.S., I found that my car was repossessed by the bank, and I had a foreclosure notice on my mortgage. Confused by what was happening, I then learned it was because my ex-husband got into my purse, took my card and emptied my bank account during the 3 months I was away and didn't leave anything to cover the payments. I was sad and more depressed to be dealing with all of this on top of my father's death. At that point, I didn't have any means of transportation to get to work or anywhere else for that matter. I called my sister and we started a pooling. Pooling is a term used when a group of people contribute a set sum of money every month so that each one of the group receives the total sum of the group's contributions. I was to get the first money and use it to buy a car so I could go to work. Indeed, I was able to buy a used car and return to work. At the same time, I contacted my mortgage company and made a deal with them to push the back payment to the end of the term and to give me a grace period to get myself back on track. I was able to readjust the mortgage after just a month. All my other bills were past due. I had a shut-off notice for the gas and the electricity. I spent a few days after coming back making phone calls to explain my situation to my utility providers but I was many months recovering from the loss of my savings that had been taken by my soon to be ex-husband.

Chapter 19

Breaking the Shackles of Abuse

The aftermath of divorce is difficult, but parents should at least try setting aside their differences in an attempt to be civil for the kids' sake. I'll be the first to admit that it's not always easy. My now ex-husband refused to play a productive role in the girls' lives as a responsible parent, making co-parenting difficult. I tried to make peace with my abuser for my kids in an attempt to co-parent with him, but his hate and anger were so strong that it blinded him from seeing that he was hurting his girls – our girls. He knew that they mean the world to me, so he used them to keep hurting me and controlling me; he couldn't see that he was hurting them in the process.

When I invited him to their school activities, he took those invitations as a sign of weakness and interpreted this as a sign that we might get back together. He never did fully understand that the moment he laid hands on me, that ship had sailed and there was nothing left to preserve.

Despite living only five minutes away, he never visited for more than a very short period of time, let alone attending any school activities like the father/daughter dance. I can't say he was a bad person from the beginning, nor will I say that he is 100% evil. I think alcoholism is partially to blame for his poor decisions, but I also believe that people have the choice to allow it to control them or not. Some people choose alcohol over their family, perhaps due to depression or the failure to see the light at the end of the tunnel. I believe that alcohol brings out a person's true colors.

I remember clearly the sad look in Malaz's eyes when her dad didn't show up for her school activities or didn't even come to visit them. He used to call her and promise to come and see them or take them places. She would get her little bag ready with all of her stuff and sit by the door. She would wait for a few hours, and then, he would call and apologize and give her a lame excuse. I could see the life get sucked out of her eyes. It hurt me to see her hurt and I felt hopeless. I didn't want to say "don't get your hopes up, so you don't get hurt" even though I knew it would have helped her. I kept watching her give him more chances and each time, he would break his promises. Malaz got older and tired of waiting so she stopped trusting him. I don't think he comprehended how smart the girls are and that they were old enough to see beyond his lies.

Children are always the innocent victims when a marriage is destroyed by abuse and alcoholism. It's impossible to protect them from this. They are witnesses to all that's happening. Their disappointments and memories will unfortunately be a part of their adult personality. They always observe far more than the abusive parent could possibly know. They miss very little and end up making their own decisions in determining guilt and blame. All the single custodial parent can do is try to minimize the damage, bolster their self-esteem, give guidance and hopefully, at some point, bring another adult into their world to prove to them that not all relationships have to be bad – not all have to be controlled by alcohol and physical abuse.

As a single mom, I had to step up and do everything. I had to be both the "good cop" and the "bad cop". I had to be firm with them and tough when needed and kind and loving, too. Seeing them cry is difficult; I felt powerless when I was unable to hug them and make them feel better. I would sometimes feel overwhelmed trying to make sure they were feeling loved, reassured, and safe when at the same time that was the only thing I needed. Witnessing the hurt in the eyes of my eldest as she realized that she was different than the kids her age was almost more than I could bear.

My youngest, on the other hand, didn't get to know him that well, except for the occasional visit, but I am sure those moments she spent with him certainly meant something to her. When she grew older, she refused to attend the father/daughter dance. A couple of my friends wanted to take her and I offered as well, but she declined. In my opinion, schools should be more sensitive when it comes to that kind of event that shines a spotlight on the loss felt by children with absent fathers (or mothers). It hurts me every year when I receive the papers from their school reminding me that the dance is "just around the corner". It makes me feel helpless and reminds me that no matter how hard I try, I can't truly take the place of a father figure in their lives. I sometimes get angry at him all over again for making my girls miss out on things, especially what he should be doing for them. He should be giving them advice on or helping them with everyday lessons. I had to come to the conclusion that I would be both parents for them.

Their disease whether it be alcoholism, drug addiction, mental disorder, physical abusers or just being the world's biggest jerk, destroys families and affects children, but it also destroys their own self-esteem and ruins their own lives. In a real way, they become victims of themselves.

Many can't handle the consequences of their own choices. They live in denial, lying to others to make themselves feel better about their own shortcomings. Some women choose to ignore all those signs for various reasons. I chose to fight against the odds, to apply myself and strive for a better life. He chose to give up, being heedless about the future. Perhaps my strength compounded his guilt about his own shortcomings, which in turn, bred resentment. Those emotions bubbled to the surface when he was drunk, and that translated to hitting, slamming doors, throwing objects and on top of that becoming verbally and emotionally abusive.

No one around me knew how bad it was until I started talking, but it was evident by then due to the visible black-and-blue marks. At that time, all I needed was someone to ask about my well-being, guide me and tell me that it would be alright. To this day, I question anything that I perceive to be out of the ordinary, since I recognize the importance of being in tune with those who are hurting. Sometimes, all someone needs to hear are words of assurance in order to be open to advice on how to leave a dangerous and harmful situation.

Unfortunately, it took more than five years to realize that I couldn't help my spouse. I needed to help myself and my kids before I ended up as another statistic. My own inability to leave gave me a better understanding as to why battered women stay and that leaving a difficult situation is often more easily said than done. It gave me an understanding that sometimes you just have to take that heavy ball and run, run, run, as fast as you can, away from all the trouble. Leaving the abuser is a huge step that must be taken.

The main reason that I speak about my issues is to inspire others. I am not ashamed to admit that I experienced domestic violence. After I fled political violence in Sudan, I thought of myself as someone who could make a difference. After all, I was a spokesperson for the Democratic Forefront in college and I fought for women's rights and equality. I battled against violence and discrimination. I immigrated to America in search of a better life, yet ended up facing violence in my own home. If this happened to me, it could happen to anyone, so I continue to fight for those who can't.

Many people wonder why I stayed so long. A common question is, "Why didn't you leave sooner?" I used to ask other victims the same question, that is, until I became one. Unfortunately, I still don't have a solid answer as it is a mix of excuses, emotions, and falling prey to false hope. Some lack confidence to swim upstream alone;

others are terrified of being lonely and are blind to the fact that staying with the wrong person amounts to a lonely existence. Some are afraid for their lives due to umpteen threats from the abuser, while others simply stay for the benefit of the children. If you meet a person who has escaped abuse, rather than questioning the timeline, consider instead praising them for having the bravery to escape. This approach means a lot to someone who is already broken and beaten, both mentally and physically. Support from society, family, and friends can mean life or death to someone. Before you judge a victim, try to see things through their eyes and put yourself in their shoes, and if you think that talking about domestic violence in the United States is taboo, consider my culture where some form of domestic abuse is not only considered normal... but often even expected. Calling the cops, or fighting in court in that type of society, only compounds the matter and earns you a "scarlet letter", so to speak.

I share my cautionary tales not to create controversy among members of my culture or family but to fight for my girls and the victims out there who lack a voice. I strive to be their voice, and I know others who share their stories in an effort to help someone who is going through a similar situation. If repeating these stories over and over can save someone's life somewhere, then it is worth it. If sharing raises community awareness, then let's share our stories to make a difference.

I advise those who are being abused to get out sooner, rather than later. In my situation, I dealt with it for years before I escaped, thinking that things would change. The longer I stayed, the longer I felt bad about myself. I felt both ashamed for staying and ashamed for trying to leave, which ironically, resulted in an endless unhealthy cycle of self-flagellation. I knew inside that I was a strong woman, so it was a shock to me to be dealing with the dichotomy of it all.

131

You try to make peace with it for some odd reason, and in my case, I tried to help him and thought I could bring about change, but that wasn't the case here. Take it from me, get out! Those who think they can change a grown man are usually sadly mistaken. An abused spouse must realize that we have mental institutions, psychologists and rehab facilities designed and created to help those who are suffering from mental instability and are in need of serious help. That spouse is not a government institution. They must stop trying to admit sick people into their lives under that pretense that they have the ability to heal those in need of professional help. An abused spouse is NOT their doctor, NOT their teacher. They do NOT have the education and emotional detachment that allows you to know how to handle their deficiencies. They cannot cure them. They are their partner – if they are not functioning at the same level as them... leave! I can say with authority, after having spoken to many survivors, if they did it once, they will do it again. Leave as soon as it starts, or you're likely to face more issues, serious injuries, and even death.

When one leaves an abusive relationship, it will be the best day of their life; I know it was for me. If you're in an abusive relationship, what have you got to lose? Take your chances, find a shelter, or seek out someone who can help, even if you have to start from ground zero. I started my life from scratch when I moved from Sudan. After the divorce, I began all over again. I lost my house and material things, but I gained my freedom, self-respect, my kids' future and my life!

I can't promise you it will be easy, but I can promise you it will be worthwhile.

It is critical to remember that your actions as a mother or a father will determine the way your children will act and how they will treat others. It will also determine how they allow others to treat them so choose wisely. If they witness their father respecting their mother, appreciating her and treating her equally, they will expect to be treated the same way. If your daughter sees you being mistreated and you are accepting it, then she will grow up thinking that this is the way it is supposed to be and will expect the same from her partner. The same applies to your son. If he witnesses inequality in the home, he will treat his partner similarly. Parents have responsibilities not just to themselves, but to the children they are raising. If we teach our boys that girls are equally intelligent and deserve fair treatment and respect, we will raise men who will view women as equals and with respect, and society will be much better for it. The double standard I witness on a daily basis is shocking. Women are guilty of this behavior as well, so it's important that they are made aware because they are the ones who are all too often raising this generation alone. You can be fairly sure that at some point they hated the same behavior they now seem to condone. The vicious cycle must be broken, even if we need to start from scratch to rise up a healthy community on our own.

We can make a difference in our community by how we raise our children and the language we use in their presence. I always say parents' involvement can make a huge difference to a young mind and affect their present as well as their future. When I see a child acting in a mean way, bullying others, I wonder what life did that child live? No one is born with hate; it is taught to them by bad experiences or being bullied themselves. Their young mind only knows what they see and experience, and they are easy to mold and shape into a great individual or a broken one. Every parent has a chance to see their kids' action and behavior if they only pay attention. It is up to them to ignore it… or take a stand. For the kids who are raised without parents, it is the society's responsibility to shape them or the foster homes, the schools and the centers they attend. Be aware of your surroundings every day, and you will see something that will make you think. Be introspective and disregard that which negatively affects you, and the world will be a better place. To change your life, you must change your surroundings by taking small steps. You have the power within you and may surprise yourself, but you have to take that first step.

My Malaz learned the meaning of responsibility at an early age, and sometimes, I feel as if she was forced to grow up too soon. She didn't have much of a childhood and had to grow up quickly to be my helper. As a single mother, I faced so many struggles. From tending to the daily needs of the kids by myself, to worrying about one of them getting sick or hurt when I wasn't there to help. Lacking a partner to help with things like picking them up from school or daycare, or if they have to leave due to sickness was a struggle. There are so many issues you face alone, from loss of income, to being judged as a bad employee for tending to your children. Choosing between your kids and your job when your kids are ill requires a delicate balancing act, since the responsibility is on you and you alone have to figure it all out while continuing to be the breadwinner. It's not easy and sometimes leads to many sleepless nights when you're spending time at hospitals and doctors' offices. Add to that all the hours you dedicate to helping out at their school, eating lunch with them, attending school activities, running around for music lessons, or sports practice – you find yourself wishing there were more hours in a day.

When I reflect back on this period of my life, I am reminded of when Remaz was a year old and I would wake my girls up to get them dressed and to daycare at 6 a.m. Malaz helped by brushing her sister's teeth at the daycare and ensuring that she ate breakfast before taking the bus to school. She was my right hand and a huge help during those busy times and learned at an early age to be responsible. She acted as a second mother to her baby sister; there was no other choice until I switched daycares and met one of the teachers there. Her name was Tiffany and she was a very unique young lady. Her personality and attitude towards life were so refreshing. Remaz got really attached to Tiffany, and Tiffany fell in love with the girls. She became their older sister and a go-to for me. Tiffany was there any time we needed her, and I didn't need to say much for her to understand when I was stressed. She used to stay with the girls so I could have some time to breathe and recuperate. She was there for their activities, all Malaz's school plays and all their birthdays. Her family became our family, and the girls were a part of their activities from that day moving on. Up to this day, even though the girls are older they still love their time with Tiffany, and I call her anytime I need advice.

Even with everything Tiffany did for our family, she was working full time and attending school at the same time. She could only do just so much in what free time she had. With Malaz now taking the bus to school, it became necessary to change daycare center to one where her bus would pick her up. This meant leaving the daycare where Tiffany worked. My work and school absolutely meant that I had to drop the girls at daycare early each morning. This new daycare was much closer to our home and actually gave me a little more flexibility. With the center closing at 6:00 P.M. it was necessary to find someone to watch the girls until I could return home – often as late as 9:00 or 10:00 P.M. I was fortunate to find another wonderful lady at the new daycare named Wafa. She spoke Arabic and was very understanding of my struggles. She offered to take the girls with her at closing and mind them until I returned. When I picked up the girls, they were well fed, happy and had been well cared for.

Wafa became a lifesaver for those times Tiffany wasn't able to help. Coincidence and convenience brought Wafa to us, and between both her and Tiffany, I was able to continue my work and studies. Once I graduated as a Registered Nurse, it became necessary to expand my support "group" as weekend and occasional overnight shifts became necessary. I'm not quick to trust my girls to just anyone. I was most fortunate that three of my friends stepped up and offered to help – Arvilla, Sara and Fatima.

Sara and Fatima were sisters and very reliable. They were willing to take turns staying overnight with the girls when necessary, and Arvilla who was also and nurse, was willing to pick up the girls in the wee hours of the morning and deliver them to the daycare. These three along with Tiffany and Wafa – joined with very few others during these hard times – provided the trustworthy support I needed to move on with my work and schooling to complete my quest for success – success in both career and family.

Without their help, my life would have been a complete disaster. With every day that passed, the girls' demands on me increased. Even with all the help I was receiving, it was hard for me to keep up with my kids, school, and work.

Chapter 20

A Single Parent Family and a Business

In the middle of all this struggling, I was lucky to find a perfect live-in nanny. Soon enough, she earned my trust with my girls after I saw how good she was with them. The girls became attached to her, especially Remaz. She followed her everywhere like her shadow. She became like a second mother to them and loved them like her own. The most important thing for me was their safety and happiness, and that's what she provided and more. Remaz learned some Arabic from her and also learned healthy eating habits. She was a very healthy woman, and that became a lifestyle in our house. She also took Malaz to her sports and activities when I was not able to do it, myself. Since Remaz was young, she played with her and took her to the park until she became old enough to attend school. She was a great help at home and took a load off my back for two years. During that time, I was able to accomplish a lot because I knew with confidence that the girls were being properly taken care of. I finished my Bachelor's degree in nursing and began my own business. Things started to fall in place, that is, until she got engaged and moved on.

Once again, I found myself keeping the balls in the air, myself, as I began the search for another nanny. I went back to the same struggle. I had to wake the girls up early to take them to a babysitter, and another sitter stayed with them after school until I arrived home from work. I worked twelve hour shifts with the commute adding an additional hour. We had a few 'not so good' babysitters who we had to let go soon after they started.

One of those horrible babysitters was an older lady who I thought would be good for the girls as she would provide a grandmother image for them. In my mind, grandmas are all kind and love kids, but this one was different – very different. She was with us for less than a week when I received a phone call only a few minutes after I had left home for work. It was Malaz and she was crying and in a complete panic. She told me that the old lady had hit Remaz on the face so hard that Remaz fell down on the bathroom floor. Remaz was under two years old!

The bathroom was tiny in this old brick house built in 1955 with two bedrooms and so little room in the bathroom that you could barely stand in front of the sink without stepping on the commode. In other words, if she struck Remaz hard enough to knock her to the floor, it was likely that she would hit either the toilet, the sink or the pipes. Fortunately, she fell towards the door – the only clear path to the floor and avoided what possibly could have been serious injury. All this was because Remaz had been using the commode and had spilled water on the floor. This old lady thought that that justified punishment and struck her there on the spot.

Obviously, I was beside myself and hung up with Malaz and had no choice but to turn around and head home. All I could think in my panic was what if she had hit her head and had sustained serious injuries – what if she had been killed??? What am I working and studying so hard for??? If it's not for those two girls??? I couldn't bear the thought of losing one of them or even seriously hurt by someone. My blood was boiling at that moment and I realized if the woman hadn't been so old, things might have been much worse. Needless to say, she was no longer in my employ. While I didn't file charges, I did tell her that there was never any justification to lay a hand on anyone, let alone a young child. I gave her money for a bus ticket home, and called her daughter and informed her of what had happened and that her mom was no longer welcome in our house. From this time on, I was much more careful about who I allowed in our home or anywhere around my kids. This made a huge impression on both girls, and they remember it to this day... especially Malaz, Remaz's second mother and protector.

I searched for a second nanny to stay with them at the house, so they wouldn't have to struggle through their entire childhood. After all, I thought, it's not their fault that their father made poor choices, or that they didn't have a "normal" family. I was never able to find another nanny that met with the children's approval, but we did meet a very special lady by the name of Heather in the process. Her son was Remaz's age, and from the first day they met, they became friends. That made it a lot easier for me to ask Heather for help when my nanny left, and she stepped up and was willing to help and take care of them. They loved her and she was able to give them things that I couldn't give them. She took them places when I couldn't be there, and she enjoyed many of the activities that the girls enjoyed. Some activities, like camping and hiking, I'm not very fond of even though the girls seemed to enjoy them. I often reminded the girls and Heather that living in Sudan was kind of like roughing it on a camping trip, and that this was a memory I felt no need to relive. Since I'm not a fan of roughing it like this and the girls seemed to enjoy it, Heather and her son allowed them to enjoy camping, but I reminded them that they could leave the campground anytime they wished. On the other hand, in Sudan I had no option to pack my bags and declare the camping trip to be over. Indeed, I experienced this hard way of living every day – day in and day out. I hiked every morning to school from first grade through college. Walking was not a choice by any means. So they had to excuse me if I didn't find "roughing it" in the wilderness as particularly interesting or even a joyful experience.

The girls found it fun to laugh and accuse me of being weak for not wanting to venture into the woods and join in their outdoor activities. She brought not only camping and hiking into their lives, but such kid activities as zoos, water parks and amusement parks became a reality. It was a great relief to me that having Heather in their life allowed them to do all of the things that her kids and others like my daughters enjoyed.

She became part of our family and was a huge part of my success today. Heather was there every day even during the summertime when they didn't have school. Even when she became pregnant, I could still count on her. I could clearly see how she felt about the girls and how the girls felt about her and her kids. With time, we grew close to her and her family, and she continues to play an important role in my life and the girls' lives. Sometimes life plays sick jokes on me, and other times, life puts people like Heather on my path to even it out. I will forever be thankful for the day I met her. She understood my struggles and had a great knowledge of the struggle that single mothers face.

Being a single mother is not an easy job especially if you are a working single mother. You are expected to give your all to your job so you can succeed in your profession and also give your all at home so your kids can succeed. For me, it wasn't just giving my all to both my kids and my profession. It was also starting my business. I faced the challenge of building it from the ground up, which also took away from family time. Making those difficult choices was a matter of survival, but with the help of a live-in nanny, I was able to move forward and concentrate on getting the business off the ground. I was in this situation because I wanted a better life for myself and my girls, a safe life. You reach the point where your entire life revolves around your kids, their needs, and their feelings. You don't want them to feel different. That makes you do more for your kids than any "normal" family does in an effort to prove to yourself or others around you that you are okay. You want your kids to feel like they aren't missing anything.

140

I found myself trying to be there for every activity, helping them to fulfill every dream that they had, and providing them with everything they wanted. I tried my best to be there and to do it for them. So many days it was impossible to leave work or stop what I was doing to simply go and watch a school play but I often did it anyway. Heather and Tiffany understood this and helped me accomplish that. I was able to manage my time and get things done and also be there for my kids. If I couldn't, Heather or Tiffany would be there.

I was a working single mother; regardless of the help I received, I still felt guilty when it came to saying no to certain things. Such as saying no to a PTO meeting or volunteering at the school; the guilt that the society puts on us is unbearable. So is the way some parents look at you, shaming you for not doing what they do. I want to say to them: please be more sensitive. Be understanding that sometimes behind that big smile facing you is a broken soul – a mother who endured domestic abuse, yet woke up every morning with a smile to shield her children from her own pain... a mother who spent all night working so she can take an hour out of her busy day to attend a school play... a mother who spent many sleepless nights thinking about when the kids' next meal will be and how to get the rent money, the car payment, the utilities and the kids' new clothes.

They don't see behind the scenes of a mother who reads to her kids at night, tends to their pain, and never complains about the load. They don't witness the acts of a mother whose love for her children is unconditional, and most definitely, they don't comprehend that single parents don't have holidays, or "days off". Regardless, they need to be up in the morning and on time for work.

They may be facing a mother who will wear used clothes from a second-hand store so her kids can wear new ones and have the book bag that every kid is talking about. Not that I am teaching them to buy expensive, materialistic things just because everyone has them, but every now and then, I let them enjoy something they really like. At the same time, I made sure that I taught them that regardless of the name brand, the shoes serve the same purpose. When I explained this to them, they became very conscious about spending. I used everything that happened to us as a teaching moment. I found using my life experience as a guide and example for the girls to be very beneficial. As a parent, that is your primary purpose – guiding your kids as they prepare to take on life's challenges.

Please talk to your kids about *you*, what you had to do as a kid and how other kids live, both in different countries and also here in the United States. Point out those who are less fortunate. You will be surprised what they will remember from that conversation and how you can influence their actions towards the world by discussing these issues.

I wanted to tell the other mothers my story and tell them how many times I had to give myself a pep talk to keep going. I often had to tell myself, it isn't easy, but it isn't impossible either. Then, I looked at the endless list of chores ranging from fixing something that is broken to doing the grocery shopping and cooking, and I could feel my stress level climbing up my body. I did it, but it took a toll on me. I often felt drained like an aged car battery. Many times, I felt like quitting. But next morning, I always realized that I had no other options but to put on a big smile and keep fighting. There are so many moments when I would just hop in my car, drive around, and cry my heart out. I found this very helpful; it helped me clear my soul and mind and gave me the energy to move forward. I think my girls only saw me crying a few times out of frustration; I kept it to myself, for the most part. I didn't want to worry them or reveal how drained I was for fear they might get the wrong idea, feel guilty and blame it on themselves – especially Malaz, since she was older than her sister, and she was there through it all.

At that time, it was hard for me to understand that it is okay to ask for help. It is ok to admit that I am a human, and although I might be strong, it's unrealistic to think I can work 24/7. I didn't feel it was okay to take time off, even if it was one hour to be by myself in an attempt to collect my thoughts and take a breather. I didn't understand the concept of "self-care". You're not able to help others if you don't take care of yourself. I know it was hard and still is hard for me to think this way. I feel guilty every time I enjoy a minute when my kids are away at school, or with friends. Mothers often are instilled with guilt that can rob us of the pleasure of alone time without our kids.

Thinking about how people would have helped me back then brings me to one specific memory. Many years ago, I was sitting in class, not listening to a word that the teacher said, when all of a sudden, my thoughts started to pour out of my eyes in the shape of tears. Little did I know that one of the students who was sitting beside me, observed my predicament. I hurried out of the room and headed to the bathroom as she followed me offering to help. She asked if I was okay, and I hesitated before I answered. How could I put my thoughts into simple words to put her mind at ease? How could I assure her that I was okay when I knew deep down that I wasn't? Would it matter at all how I responded? By the time I reached a decision on what to say, the class was over and the students flooded into the hall. I responded that I was okay and then walked away.

Years passed and a similar thing happened to me, only this time I was the observer. I saw a young lady sitting with the same sad look of despair in her watery eyes. Quietly, I sat by her side, thinking of myself in the same situation. What was it that I needed to hear at the time? I thought that perhaps I could do something to help. I started talking about when I was in class and how I wish that I had told the stranger that I wasn't okay and that I needed to open up and allow someone in. How therapeutic it would have been to vent and let some of those emotions out to release the pressure that can sometimes cause us to explode! After that, I sat quietly and asked her if she was okay. I never knew how powerful those three words were until I heard the sounds of the young lady sobbing. I asked myself if I crossed the line by opening up the emotional floodgates. I questioned if I could handle her issues on top of mine, but sometimes we need to think of others before we think of ourselves. She took a deep breath and poured out her soul. I will never forget that moment and how it made me feel. Words starting flowing and we sat there for more than two hours talking. The change in her emotions, her eyes and her attitude after getting it all out made me think. Was that so hard to do? It took a couple hours of my time, but it probably gave her back a couple of years or at the very least, made her feel like she wasn't alone. I share this story to encourage you to be ready to listen to others. The next time you ask someone if they're ok, be sure to mean it and give them time to think and realize that they aren't alone. You don't know the power of those three words until you've opened the gate.

My personal battle has given me the opportunity to better understand the struggle that a wide range of women have to encounter throughout their lives and how difficult it sometimes is for us, as people, to make decisions that are healthy and beneficial to us. I look back and wonder how many times did I let other people influence and dictate my decisions? How many times did I find excuses for my abuser and try to help him? How many times was I scared to make the right decision for fear of the unknown? I soon found myself with a newfound clarity that led me to fathom the importance of guiding others who have experienced a similar situation.

Those facing comparable issues must be brave enough to face their abusers, many of whom are persistent in their harassment long past the breakup. The fear of retaliation, the fear of death threats and the lies they threaten to spread can be overwhelming. The worst part is that the abuser is intimately aware of your weaknesses and will attempt to use them against you. Those facts taunted me for a long time, and they were some of the reasons I was reluctant to let someone else into my life.

Chapter 21

Growing and Evolving - Life Goes on for All

I was once sitting in my car in a pharmacy parking lot when an elderly couple caught my attention. They were holding hands – he steadier than she. He walked to her side, opened the car door, helped her in, and closed the door. He walked to his side and settled in behind the wheel. I am sure that if the situation was different and she was steadier than him, then she probably would've helped him to his side and behaved in the same manner. This is the difference between someone who was raised with respect and taught how to give and accept it. It might be an ordinary action for them, but it was big for me. This common but beautiful gesture happens all the time between many old couples, and it really made me wonder how this generation could be so occupied with violence, the degradation of women, the lack of respect for the elderly and each other.

It got me to reflect back on my failed relationship and the time I wasted thinking that we might grow old together and enjoy the little things in life. When I see older couples holding hands, just sitting and enjoying each other's company, I feel robbed of that experience of having someone to lean on. Then, I remembered that if we don't walk the path we are given, we might never find out how it ends. That's why when I am asked what I think of marriage and relationships after my experience, I respond that it's better to be alone than with someone who can make you feel alone, and that's how it is if you have nothing in common or he/she doesn't fulfill your needs. I sometimes ask myself if I'd be happier alone, or with someone who fails to respect me... and then, the answer is clear. Am I open to finding a partner in the future? Sure, but until I meet the one who can fulfill my needs and expectations, I will continue down my own path, alone and happy. You are the one who has to be content with your decisions in life and nothing will make sense if you are dissatisfied with your choices.

Rushing from one failed relationship to another is a huge problem in my view. Some of us were made to believe that you need a man, or a woman, to be happy. I say you need to know yourself and love yourself to find that elusive emotion that we call happiness. Recognize what you can give to others and determine what your individual needs are before you jump into a relationship.

Humans are simple, yet complicated. I wrestle with so many mixed emotions about relationships and life itself, and every time I think I've mastered the game of life, I realize that I am far from figuring things out. Many times at night, when I am still, I reflect back and wonder how I've gotten to this point. So many decisions led me to where I am today. Some I consider right and others wrong. Would it be fair to assume that I learned many lessons through these experiences? If I chose a different path, would it have led me to a better result? Or maybe just to a different road? I wonder about these things we call "choices". Do we enjoy misery? Do we look for hard, unpaved roads just for the adventure? Is there any easy path? If so, what does that look like?

I've had my share of failed relationships, for many reasons. I sometimes wondered if I would ever find the right one, but I knew he is out there. I often questioned if our paths would meet before it is too late, or would we already have passed each other in a parallel universe? Those questions crossed my mind and then life happens, I got busy again with work and other responsibilities and I forgot about my love life for a while.

It took time for me to admit that I, too, deserved a break, and in order for me to continue on a positive path, I needed a warrior's rest. As I contemplate the future, I realize that, at some point, I will need a partner, someone to love and be loved by. I would try to give myself pep talks in order to allow other people to get to know me, but it wasn't easy. Once you reach a certain point in your life and you find your comfort zone, it is hard to allow someone else to enter your circle. I often felt as if allowing someone to enter my life would be a burden. I spent a long time getting to know and love who I am, and I believe when you know your worth, and you are satisfied with what you have, you don't need anyone else to justify your existence. When you are satisfied with your accomplishments and when you know that you are capable of doing anything and everything, you will become content with your life. Sometimes I think I've reached a point where I'd rather stay alone than be with the wrong person. I believe that the more successful the person, the harder it is for her/him to settle down or to remain in a relationship. You realize that you don't need a man/woman to make you happy. You learn how to love yourself and not apologize for your success and strength. At that time, when you look for a partner, you will look for someone to complement you. You will look for a boyfriend or a husband to match your personality, behavior, thoughts and interests.

For me, my choice will be someone I can relate to, talk to – someone to complement me mentally, emotionally and sexually – to bring out the best in me and allow me to grow. Understand that I say complement, not complete. I don't like the word complete. When someone says I need someone to *complete* me, I want to advise them against using that terminology and help them to understand that if they are missing something in their life, that they need to find it first before putting that burden on someone else. We really shouldn't rely on anybody else to validate our existence. People make the mistake of entering into a relationship and thinking that the other person will fill the void that they are missing, that they will bring them the happiness and joy they are looking for. Unfortunately, that's not what happens. They still feel that emptiness but have brought another party into the problem. The unhappiness usually tends to put a strain on the relationship, ultimately ending it. Any relationship that doesn't add some kind of value to your life ends up stunting your growth, and in the end really isn't a healthy relationship. Most people are intuitive that way and understand when things just aren't quite right. Our gut instinct often guides us to the truth, yet we reject it. Do we, sometimes, unintentionally jeopardize our happiness?

Many times I asked myself those same questions while contemplating my path. I stayed single for several reasons. First of all, I was comfortable with the life I had created. I was taking my time to know and love myself and experience many things and emotions in life. I was also at the stage where I felt like those whom I met didn't have what it took to complement me – the potential partners that I had met and considered didn't seem quite equipped to rise to the occasion. When I compared my life to what I thought they could bring to the table, I came to the conclusion I was better off without them.

One thing that continued to hinder my happiness and make my decision to stay single a little bit challenging was how society viewed single mother divorcees – as if being a single mother is a liability, a bad thing, a failing, a shortfall. In my case, few people took the time to ask me how I am feeling and if I am okay and happy being single. Many just assumed you are broken and miserable. We single mothers in turn often felt the need to mask our feelings which doesn't help matters. Any emotion you show can translate into something else. If you are sad, it's because you are single. If you cry, that means you are weak, and for that reason, I kept my weak moments to myself. It makes you feel as if you are under a microscope at all times. You are expected to do things in certain ways. It can be a lot of pressure.

149

On top of the societal pressure, single mothers have to deal with some sick men out there who view them as an easy target. I don't understand where this idea came from, but some men tend to view divorced women as vulnerable and therefore easy prey. Many can be judgmental, viewing us as having failed at marriage, and in the back of their minds, they attribute fault to the woman automatically, instead of questioning the reason why. We teach the new generations not to give up and that it is okay to fail, but marriage has a double standard attached to it.

With all the experiences and the hardships that I endured, I am prepared to move on with my life. I don't let the negatives control my thoughts, but I am also not naive anymore. I know there will be trials and tribulations. But there is one thing I know for sure: I will be fine... regardless. I sometimes overanalyze everything which is not good in any relationship. I am aware of that, but some habits die hard. Some might view my opinions as being too pessimistic, but given what you have read about my history, you now understand why I can't let my guard down, even for a minute. Despite all this, I still view my glass as half full.

Chapter 22

Glass Half Full – Family Life with Twists

By viewing the glass as half full, I realize that everything bad that happened to me made me strong and who I am today. If one good thing can come out of my misery and one person hears my message and survives, then my mission will be complete. Even during the worst times, I came to know many wonderful people who were there for me, and I believe they were put there for a reason and am thankful for each and every one of them. Each day I wake up with a smile and live my life as it is meant to be lived. I think of what I can do to help others, and I am determined to make it a great day, regardless of what's going on. No matter what life hurls in my direction, I make it a point to keep my head up and walk to my destination with a smile. It's really about perception and I view it as a challenge. I find simple things in life to enjoy, or use as a stress reliever – many of which bring joy to my heart from watching my girls pursuing their dreams, to the simple pleasures of traveling down the highway with my daughters in the car – windows down, music playing and the wind messing up my hair. It never fails to put a smile on my face. Find what brings a smile to your face and embrace and treasure it. I always say family, music and good friends make this life tolerable, and I am thankful to have an amazing family and so many good friends.

Life is gradually growing easier for the girls and I. Many years ago the girls started showing interest in acting and modeling and I supported their interest. I contacted a few agencies, and as with so many other things in life, you live and learn. The first two agents I dealt with turned out to be scammers, so we ended up taking two steps backwards before moving forward. As a result, I learned to do my research before accepting and signing any contracts.

I took days off work to drive them to New York City and back – sometimes in the same day! We have it down to a science – everyone chooses a row. Our vehicle has three rows and we take blankets, pillows, activity books and a change of clothes and we're good to go. They know that I will support their dreams and will do anything in my power to help them attain them.

This is a hobby for Malaz. Her main focus is on her education. She is an honor student, a very talented, smart, well-rounded young woman. If she stays focused, she will achieve all of her goals. Remaz also loves school very much and she is into music. She plays piano, violin and French Horn. She has a beautiful voice and is taking voice lessons. She, too, is a well-rounded girl who will have a bright future if she stays focused. Once we found a legitimate agency, work began pouring in, and suddenly, we were traveling from Pennsylvania to New York every week – sometimes twice a week. It was very tiring and time-consuming and most certainly a challenge, but it made them happy and gave them the opportunity to explore their talents and view various options. This unique journey taught them how to respect time and the art of preparing for an audition, which will come in handy as they strive to excel in everyday life. These experiences also help them learn that there is no limitation to what they can do, as long as they follow their dreams and work hard for them.

Both of the girls accepted several acting jobs, and it soon became too difficult for us, after three years of continuous driving to New York and back. Remaz appeared on Sesame Street, which was a dream come true for her (and me, for that matter). To be on the set of a childhood show that shaped all our lives and to interact with the characters was the highlight of her day. She was all smiles when Elmo and Abby complimented her hair and called her "Rapunzel".

Remaz was also on set for few commercials. One commercial never did make it to air, but it was a valuable and unique experience for her, especially the part where she had the opportunity to have her hair done and be dressed by her own personal stylist. She is my little princess, and I was happy that the experience made her feel so special. She also did a great job as the lead on a Dorito commercial and accepted a small part on a movie about bullying. Malaz was in a few movies as well as an extra playing a bully and a dinner guest. She also modeled in an NFL jersey catalog photo shoot. They worked together in tandem on a few projects I believe that brought them closer together. Malaz was always Remaz's second mom. She helped her with everything including memorizing lines with her, coaching her on how to act, and more.

The girls missed so many days at school. Although the teachers knew they could be trusted to keep up with their homework on the road, it was physically tiring for them and me, too. Soon, the exhaustion became too much to bear, and it adversely affected other areas of our lives. I eventually, came to realize that I needed to redirect my focus on my business, and they, in turn, needed to redirect their focus on school. Remaz dislikes missing school; she has a unique relationship with her teachers and enjoys all her classes. She especially hates missing lunch when they have mac and cheese. I couldn't understand her fascination with her school lunch. She would get really sad when we would have to drive to New York during the school day and especially if we had to leave before lunch. Malaz, on the other hand, had difficulty missing school because she is in the gifted program, and all her classes are either honor or AP classes. This put pressure on her when she would miss classes, and she would have to work extra hard to catch up on what she missed. We finally reached a point where we decided we all needed a break, so we contacted their agents and informed them of the decision.

They will miss a lot but sometimes, you need to know when it's time to stop spreading yourself so thin. We are glad to have been part of this experience, and during this time, we met many fascinating people, some who became good friends with me and the girls.

I admit that I grew to develop a love-hate relationship for New York City. I loved that melting pot feeling, the accessibility to everything and the ebullient feeling you get when you are part of the liveliness of the city and the street scenes.

Conversely, I began to hate the incessant traffic and bad smell that linger in the air – a putrid mixture of sewage, trash and sweat. I can't say that I minded the overcrowding, but you pay the price of getting stuck for an hour just sitting in traffic and not moving an inch. One time it took us an hour to move from one traffic light to another. I would sit there in my car watching the traffic light change from green to yellow then red and vice versa for close to an hour at times. Thankfully, I was able to use those trips as therapy and thinking time. When I am driving and listening to music, I'm essentially at peace, even when I am troubled. Sometimes, I miss those moments. It's funny how you can discover so many things about yourself in a four-hour car ride. Those times were not just therapeutic for me, but also helped the girls and I forge an even closer relationship. Being in a confined space for eight hours a day, helped us to really make the best of things and in the end, learn more about each other. We talked, sang, fought and when they were tired, they just fell asleep in the back seat. I found myself glancing at them in the rear-view mirror, and it never failed to bring a smile to my face. When they would fall asleep, I would retreat to my mind's corner and reflect back on my life and view how far I've come. Life is unpredictable and if someone had foretold my story years early, I would've thought they were exaggerating.

It wasn't all business when it came to the girls and my relationship. We had our daily routine of games and fun activities. It wasn't a set schedule; we just made the best out of the little time that we had until I was able to be there all the time. We traveled a lot. We danced to the dance games, actually they danced and followed directions, and I did whatever like my youngest always says... with a laugh. They called me silly or crazy sometimes because: I am spontaneous, I laugh loud, I sing loud and I dance all the time... and anywhere. Now that they are almost grown, they say I embarrassed them. My youngest often said that's why we shouldn't go in public with you... as they both smile and laughed.

Deep down I know they loved their crazy mama. Sometimes, you have to find what makes you happy and brings smile into your face. When you find it, don't let go; use it to improve your life and the life of the ones you love. We found what made us happy, and we used it every day. I played with my girls... any game that made them laugh. I taught them how to play cards, and they taught me their games. We often played in the car, games that we made up or just the simple I spy until they got too old for that game. We continue telling jokes and singing out loud. One of our routines is to talk about their day when they get home from school. That helped me know how their day went and gave an opportunity to get close to them. A few times here and there, I used what happened in their day as a teaching moment. It also showed them that I cared, and it taught them they can come and talk to me about anything. I do indeed, talk to my girls about anything and everything. I used every opportunity to explain to them the things I learned from my experiences, and I give them a chance to tell me what they think. It is important to have a close relationship with your kids. It gives them security and it gives you a better understanding to what is going on in their head. I am a firm believer in nurture. When you encourage the development of your kids and care for them, you will create a healthy environment for them to grow and become the best they can be.

The girls are busy doing the things that they love and enjoy, and I am enjoying watching them grow and lend them a hand when needed. I always tell them to believe in themselves and their ability to create a future full of possibilities. I assure them that doors will open if they do their best. We used to believe that the sky was the limit when it came to potential, but that's no longer true when you consider that there are footprints on the moon and other planets. The Travel to New York City required flexibility, and the only reason I was able to make their dreams come true is because of the kind of work that I did. I taught my girls what dreams are made of, and more important, I taught them that dreams are achievable through hard work, perseverance and education. I taught them to look for the own clouds to climb on and float through life – successfully.

Chapter 23

Hagir Elsheikh - A Promise for the Future

Because I worked as an agency nurse for many years, I was able to set my own schedule. The flexibility made it easy for me to schedule the days I could work especially as a single mother. It gave me the freedom to schedule around my girls' activities, doctor's appointments and all their growing needs. I was able to be there when they needed me, and that made me excel at my work, gave me a good reputation and built solid working relationships that enabled me to always find work as a full-time employee. Some of the issues that I faced as an agency nurse were my employer's inability to understand my needs, my situation and grammar added "that" they didn't have a close communication. I felt I was just a number to them. That experience and my knowledge of this type of work made me realize that I can run my own show and make a difference in the process by starting an agency that understands its employees and one which can be sensitive to their unique situations. Opening a staffing agency was one of my dreams, and when I envisioned this business, I saw a different kind of environment than the one I experienced. I envisioned an agency that offers more than a job to its employees. I was able to use my experience as a guide when it came to problem-solving... from finding a suitable babysitter, to having plan B just in case your babysitter canceled, to creating an open communication with the employees and helping them find a solution to some problems that might arise and affect their performance. Helping with those problems wasn't hard for me, since I can relate to their situation.

I believe that we, as individuals, should always be growing and evolving. Starting my own company was a dream. I didn't quite know how and where to start, but I believed in my own ability to learn and was confident in my will to fight and beat any odds. I started by going online and finding resources and phone numbers – anything to put my feet on the right path.

By researching, I was able to navigate the legal waters to start my business. From that point on, things started to fall into place. The problem was finding the financial capital to get the business off the ground. Since I had bad credit, it was not only difficult to hire and pay employees, but also to secure a business loan, so I decided to work by myself until I was able to hire and pay my employees. The first door I attempted to open was shut in my face, which was disheartening, but I kept reminding myself that I could do it. Six months passed with no activity. People who knew me and what I was capable of opened my eyes to the ugliness that existed in some that I had considered friends. I faced many obstacles and yet, I was determined to persevere.

The day finally came when I secured my first contract with a facility and began working there every day. This allowed me to save money and use my tax return to pay another employee to join me. Acquiring that first contract bolstered my confidence and trust in myself, so I began following up with other facilities until I landed the second contract, and from that point on, I was able to hire more nurses.

As a young entrepreneur, money was always a struggle. The facilities have 30 to 90 days to pay, and I pay my employees every week. I worked day and night to keep this going. Sometimes, I didn't have enough money to pay my rent, but I wasn't going to let this stop me from dreaming. A huge opportunity opened up, and those in charge learned about my agency from others who praised the quality of the service we provide. We began growing at a fast pace. Still, money was an issue. I tried anything and everything, but progress in the money arena moved at a snail's pace. I was working way harder and bringing home less money than when I worked as a bedside nurse – a job which I loved.

Being a bedside nurse taught me a lot. The feeling that you can make a difference in someone's life, or just make someone who is suffering smile is very gratifying and gave me a great deal of satisfaction. I could see myself doing it all day, every day and just as I affected their lives, they affected mine. They gave me a different perspective on life, allowing me to realize that my issues can't compare to their health struggles. At least I can take a deep breath when I want to and walk, talk and feed myself. I learned to take one day at a time. I owe my patients a lot for that. Many have told me how I made a difference in their hospital experience – how my demeanor, attitude and singing gets them through their stay and keeps their mind from dwelling on their medical issues. I understand that everyone has his or her own issues, which is why I knew it was important to leave my troubles at home to better focus on others and whatever tasks I may be tackling.

I try to remind myself every day to check my emotions and my home issues with my jacket and purse. To my surprise, people notice, and I hear a lot of good things from both my patients and their family members. I believe if you can step back and objectively view others, you may just be surprised to learn just how lucky you are compared to those who may be carrying even more baggage. I tell stories about my life and the hard times I've endured in hopes that it will motivate and help someone to understand that things could, indeed, be worse. I've worked with many clients through the years, providing them with the best services and help when they needed me. If I don't have staff to cover a shift, I cover that shift myself. I am passionate about helping others and have enough experience and wisdom to share. I feel I can contribute in many ways and believe in leading by example.

In retrospect, I am grateful for my struggle, because it made me who I am today. It also taught me that there is nothing I can't do and nothing is impossible, as long as I am willing to try as hard as I can. Giving up easily is not an option – I learned that while hanging from a tree outside a ghost house in Khartoum. Sometimes, all you need to hear is a positive word from someone else when you are down. I always try to wear my smile and influence others to be positive and kind. Kindness can go a long way and can bring joy and peace to you and your surroundings. That feeling of appreciation meant a lot to me, and when a patient's family member informed me that they were nominating me as "an inspirational woman", and that a documentary was going to be done covering my life story. Co-workers, family, friends and a patient family member participated in that documentary. It ultimately inspired me to do more good in my life. It made me feel that everything I did, and am continuing to do, is achieving its purpose – to inspire more people to do good and make a difference in their surroundings, regardless of what's going on around them.

I felt validated in my effort to make a difference in people's lives. I also viewed it as an opportunity to be able to truly make an impact on other women by taking them on a journey through my life and what it took to get to this point – through all its twists and turns, torture, trials, tragedies and finally the support of family, my beautiful children and my successes.

To hear my friends talk about how my strength gives them hope to continue fighting, gives me the courage to continue sharing my story. Some people around me wonder how I do it all and still keep a smile on my face and joy in my heart. I want them to know that life is complicated, but I choose to live, smile and cry if I have to. Occasionally, I complain to my friends and family, but it never occurs to me to give up. That award gave me the assurance to know that I am doing something right and that I don't have to be perfect. All I need to be is happy and satisfied with my life and my choices. If I can make a difference in just one person's life, then I believe I achieved my purpose. If I can show even one person how I used my strength to help me build my life and assist others, I'm on the right path. At that time, I was able to reflect on my life, assess my strengths and abilities and realize that I would be able to succeed in anything I want and can dream of.

I know I had a rough road, and part of my purpose in documenting my life is to guide my girls and others – to help them avoid the mistakes I made. It's my desire to assist them in taking a smoother path. It is their choice to take my advice or not. I am not trying to use my experience as a map they need to follow, but as a big picture they can use as a guide. It would help if I knew where each road might lead to in advance, but that's not how it works. If you know yourself well enough, you will understand your capabilities. Life can take on some surprising twists and turns, and it's up to us to overcome the obstacles. I offer my life story as an example to encourage others to believe in themselves and know that everything is possible.

My passion is to make a difference in someone else's life and to help others build a strong community that respects one another's differences and cares about each other's well-being. I want to inspire and empower others, especially women, and to assure them that there is a way out of any challenging situation, whether they be domestic violence issues, money struggles, societal pressure, or family strife. I like to believe that anyone can do it with the right mindset. Inspiring others can come in many forms; it can simply be by sharing your story, your struggles, and how you managed to overcome your obstacles.

I've had many doors closed in my face. More, in fact, than I can count. I hit rock bottom, but got back up and continued. I had no other choice; I had people depending on me. I understand that not everyone is as fortunate as I am to have a good support system, but as long as you have yourself and are willing to fight for what you believe, you will make it. That's why I always tell my girls that life is what you want it to be. There will always be struggles and hard times, but you have to keep your head held high and aim even higher.

I had a rough life, full of ups, downs, failures and achievements. What can I say? That's just life and it's expected. The best part is always waking up knowing that I have it in me to fight and keep going, but I didn't let it get me down or break me. I always viewed the glass as half full and worked to change the negatives into positives, keeping in mind that there are those who are struggling more than me. I consider myself fortunate enough to have been given a second chance in life. I benefited from trying again and knowing that if I fail to reach my dreams, I can always start over tomorrow. To me, success and doing well doesn't necessarily translate to money, although you need it to pay the bills. If you have morals and follow them and practice what you preach, then you are successful. To excel in life or in your business, it's important to give the people around you your undivided attention. Today the hard work is beginning to pay off as my girls and I work towards an ever-brighter future.

My business life, on the other hand, keeps me busy, and I strive to better myself and improve my performance every day. That being said, it was difficult to give it my all when I was on the road all the time. When we took a break, I was able to expand my business and put more time into volunteering. Running a successful business is a rewarding feeling, but it comes with a huge price. I had to put my personal life on hold, by choice for the most part. I really didn't have time to feel like I was missing something, and I think this is a situation that almost all the successful, hard-working business people deal with. It is a choice and sometimes you have to sacrifice in order to reach your goal.

Chapter 24

Sudan – The 2018/2019 Revolution

Ahmed Elkheir was a teacher in a school in Sudan. He was arrested at home, taken to a ghost house and was tortured. Unfortunately, Ahmed was well known to the security forces from previous protests. They knew him as a defiant teacher and activist leader. He was sodomized with a sharp object until he was dead. Although quite dead, they feared he was faking or just unconscious and those in charge ordered him electrocuted to make sure he was really dead. After slapping him until they were certain of their success, he was taken to a government doctor and a fake death certificate reporting that he died of poisoning was prepared. His family was very vocal and they released the body to the family – which allowed for a thorough evaluation and the confirmation of the actual cause of death. When the true nature of Ahmed Elkheir's death was known and word spread, the people angrily took to the streets again with a renewed fervor.

At the same time, two others were arrested and tortured to death and buried without their family's knowledge. This was done as a reaction to the further protests over Elkheir's torture and to further cover up the nature of their death. Up until today, the death toll from the 2018/2019 peaceful protests in Sudan is over fifty-five. We know that for sure. Another unidentified body was found on the street and clearly, that person was also tortured to death. These incidents are being repeated over and over every day in Sudan, so the final total will no doubt continue to rise and be much higher before publication.

A few other detainees were tortured and released to allow them to tell their story of depravity as a warning to others. They were held and starved, not even given water. Then, they were beat from head to toe. When each finally fell to the floor, three men took turns sodomizing them in front of others who cheered on the depraved. When they had completed their deed of total submission and the worst possible humiliation, they were released. As word spread of their fate, rather than act as a warning – this angered the protesters further and gave rise to even more taking to the streets.

As of this writing, we know of over 3000 detainees and many others uncounted for. We have seriously injured protesters who can't get the medical help they desperately need. The Sudanese government is still using live ammunition against unarmed protesters. Snipers continue to kill and wound at will. There have been incidents of multitudes being killed or injured simply by being run down by police cars. They are throwing tear gas inside protester's homes. They have thrown teargas into hospitals who attempt to give aid to protesters. The world must recognize what's happening and take action. The situation there has deteriorated to become one of the worst human rights violations anywhere in the world.

As despots and dictators are prone to do, they are targeting the educated, the professionals; they are killing doctors (a precious human commodity in any 3rd world country) for simply helping the injured protesters. The violence and sodomizing of teachers is intended as a warning for any teacher who refuses to teach only the curriculum approved by the government. They are going after any lawyers who are willing to defend the victims. This is systematic extermination carried out by the few radical Islamists who came into power via a military coup in 1989, and they are still in power to this day – against the will of the Sudanese people.

In 2013, a revolution began, and the government killed over 200 young protesters point blank – with no hesitation. That scared the people and there was only sporadic resistance through till December of 2018. Even the frightened, the downtrodden, the oppressed – all of humanity eventually reaches a breaking point. Revolution and death and injury have returned to Sudan (not that it ever really left).

***

Other than my personal struggles as a teen and young adult, I had not planned on getting into all of this in this book. This was intended to be all about my story – my struggles, my tortures, my journey to freedom and being safe from all abuse, one of providing a loving and prosperous home for my family. Indeed, one of survival. I had hoped and still do hope that by sharing my often tragic circumstances, I just might help some who are struggling. I just might make a difference in their lives. To do this properly, we had best give you a little bit of historical reference. Further on, you will find a timeline from when Great Britain shed its Sudanese colony in North Africa in 1956 until the present, but a basic understanding is required to fully absorb what's happening there. You will also find a report of recent meetings with members of the United States Congress. I joined with others in trying to enlighten them to the inhumanity that life has deteriorated to under the current Conservative Islamic Government of Sudan. You see, I cannot ignore what is happening. People are dying; I can't ignore events happening today in the country of my birth, but first some facts.

Sudan, as a former colony of Great Britain, uses the Arabic language, but many remember the English of colonial times. Arabic and English are still both the official languages. The bulk of Sudan is mostly Muslim while the far South is 97% Christian – in large part, Roman Catholic. Additionally, there are significant groups who still subscribe to both the languages and religions of their African, indigenous forefathers. Many of these indigenous peoples are located in the notorious Darfur Region of Western Sudan. Having three religiously dedicated factions trying to blend into one homogenized country was a war waiting to happen. War came quickly and ferociously to this young country.

I'll let you follow the timeline further on, but the key to what's happening today is the current Islamic Regime of Al-Bashir and his Islamic Front Organization who came to power via military coup in 1989. Basically, he is a dictator – a murderer and fascist hiding behind Sharia Law which allows the government to maintain control through vicious, bloodthirsty domination. By claiming to be a Conservative Sharia Muslim advocate, Al-Bashir has been supported for decades by a coalition of unlikely "brothers" whose only common denominator is advocating Sharia Law. While this group includes allies of the United States like Saudi Arabia, it also includes groups like Al Qaeda, ISIS and the Muslim Brotherhood.

Al-Bashir is like a cross between the vicious dictator Saddam Hussein and the religious fanatic Osama Bin Laden. He can imitate either depending on which is to his advantage – bloodthirsty warlord or conservative advocate of Sharia Law who feels death and destruction are acceptable as jihad – whichever suits his needs. But they can't hide behind this false piety. These are the same people who traffic in human beings and even steal sex slaves from other countries – while demanding total servitude of their women. These are the same people who treat women as property. These are the same people who would kill a young girl who has been raped – because rape must always be the fault of the female. These are the same people who would give one hundred lashes of the whip to a citizen caught having a drink of alcohol but would secretly have some of the finest wine cellars in the world hidden on their estates. These are the same people who mutilate female children to ensure they could not find pleasure in adult sex. These are the same people who if a girl should attempt to avoid an arranged marriage would perform what they call an "honor killing" of the young female and would go unpunished for murder. These are those who believe that cutting off hands and feet, beheadings, tying gays to a chair and throwing them off the highest building in the city are all acceptable forms of punishment, necessary because Sharia Law demands it.

After he had control of Sudan and its people, Al-Bashir's first chore was to convert the Christians in the South. War there was a constant for years between South Sudan and the government in Khartoum. After all, Sharia Law says that one must follow the Muslim Religion or they are better off dead. The easiest way to kill multitudes of infidels is to have a war – using modern weapons of warfare bought and paid for with Arab money against poorly equipped and equally poorly trained Christians. However, religion is a strong motivator on all sides and war dragged on and on. Of course, the civilian population and especially their children suffer the most in any war-torn area. With all this support, why would Al-Bashir enter the 21st century by agreeing to negotiate for peace with South Sudan? Actually, it's quite simple. In 1999, OIL was discovered in the southern regions of extremely poor Sudan. War was interfering with the ability to extract that oil and sell it at great profit for Khartoum and of course for its leaders. This made negotiating financially logical, and through 2003 and several failed attempts, the war was halted, South Sudan recognized and oil exploitation could continue in Sudan without the worry of war. Money flowed into Khartoum from the likes of Canada, Sweden and China. All adherence to the inherent rights of all people seem to take a back seat when the oil money flows. At this time, South Sudan still functions as an independent nation functioning under the current Roman Catholic President.

At the same time oil was found in 1998, the United States discovered that a chemical plant belonging to the government of Sudan but probably in conjunction with terrorists (Al Queda?) was most likely producing chemical weapons. This plant was destroyed by a U.S. airstrike and sanctions were put on the Khartoum government. Pressure from the outside combined with the promise of Oil riches, all added to the incentive to end the war in the South. It should be noted that after 9/11, the U.S. and other countries increased their sanctions on the Islamic Regime in Khartoum. This whole war area, as well as the new oil fields, is not far from where I spent my young years in Tandalti.

Al-Bashir and his thugs are religious only by convenience. They have shown their true ruthlessness on numerous occasions. He is not a legally elected President, but more of a Warlord who is intent only on preserving his domination, his corruption, his spiraling personal wealth, and quite frankly, doesn't care what must be done or who must die to achieve these goals. Whether it was assisting with the assassination of Egyptian Prime Minister Mubarak, performing genocide on the masses of poor indigenous peoples of Darfur, bombing the Christians in South Sudan or hanging a young teenage girl from a tree and beating her nearly to death – causing her great injury and months of recovery – Al-Bashir and this thugs masquerading as security forces and hiding out in Ghost Houses… function at will in their determination to maintain the status quo that has existed all these many years.

The free world – other than an occasional speech by such notables as Colin Powell blaming the regime of genocide, much lip service in the United Nations and around the world and one United States bombing that was little more than a slap on the wrist – serving notice that "if he goes too far, the U.S. will take notice" (but what is too far when his atrocities are being paid for by important allies of the United States?) – little has been done around the world to stop one of the world's greatest criminals.

Despite my personal successes here in the United States, my wonderful chosen home; despite my family responsibilities; despite the demands of my business; despite my commitment to the fight for women's rights; despite my work to eradicate domestic spousal abuse. Despite all going on in my life, I cannot ignore what is happening in the land of my birth. Human beings are dying. The WORLD must stand up and take notice.

The memory of my father and his struggle to save and serve the people of Sudan requires that my siblings and I bring the truth to the world. I can only hope that we all continue to make him proud as we continue his life of advocacy for the oppressed, his life of service to the people of Sudan.

I have joined others and brought our knowledge of what is currently happening in Sudan to Washington. We met with members of Congress and brought them facts and evidence. My brother Rashid has done the same in his chosen home country of Great Britain. You have read about what a wonderful man my brother Diaa is and all he did to help me through my tortures and finally my escape. Twice in recent weeks Diaa has survived being wounded by government forces. He is in imminent danger. Yet, he too, can no longer remain silent. And, what about Rashid and I? While we continue to deliver our message of truth around the world, Sudan state television as recently as February 2019 made it clear that were Rashid or Hagir Elsheikh to return to their country of birth, they would face execution. It would appear our words of truth are being heard somewhere. In the Appendix, you will find a synopsis of our recent meetings in Washington and a historical timeline of the recent history of Sudan. I was privileged to attend and speak along with several other activists. See Appendix for additional information.

Chapter 25

The Present

As you have read, being the spouse of an abusive alcoholic and the effect that relationship had on both myself and our daughters has been a critical part of my story. I hope that sharing my experiences might in some small way help others. I have given sound advice based on experience and remain passionate about actively pursuing the war against spousal abuse. However, I am a woman. While motherhood remains the paramount event in my life and the children remain my primary concern, they are walking steadily – no – running fast towards that time when they will escape the safety of my home and move on to make their own lives. All too soon they will be gone from my home. As a woman, I have passion and a need for companionship that grows as I realize just how close Malaz and Remaz are to beginning their adult lives.

While I now know that my relationship with my ex was in many ways a mistake, I still am thankful for my two loves that the relationship gave me. There was one relationship that began before I married which ended in a distant relationship that went on for over twenty years, but before I married and relocated to America, he immigrated to Australia where he eventually married. A few years ago, he divorced and we actually met in Dubai. We considered a relationship, but partially due to distances and certainly somewhat due to my still being in recovery mode from my own experiences, it was not to be.

Sometime later at a friend's wedding, I met someone upbeat and fun to be around who is also kind, sweet, and open-minded. He is full of life and knows how to make me laugh. I felt he would add to my life. It helped a lot that the girls fell in love with him as well. Seeing them happy is all I am asking for. I know they are worried about me and they want to see me happy. Watching him being there for them, joking, laughing together is the highlight of my day. They also have become a part of his family.

Not too long after we met, I knew I wanted to build a life with him. Although we are very dissimilar in our history, we share much in common on how we wanted to spend the rest of our lives. We soon became engaged and began planning a wedding. Though all this happened fairly quickly, we were married. I'm thrilled to be with this person, and I look forward to a brighter future with him by my side and am encouraged by the love and strength he can bring to my daughters. Of course there are no guarantees in life, but we all are enjoying a far more normal family situation.

My husband, Hazim Meshawi has never been married before. Despite being a little old for such things, we did make a conscious decision to allow our family to grow – if it should happen. As I put the final "touches" on my life's story, I can now share with you that while I write these words, I am now with child. Soon, Remaz and Malaz will have a young sibling to dote on and spoil. We are all most excited.

***

I am thankful that I was raised in a large, nurturing, supportive family that taught me to be responsible. My parents believed in equality and fairness among the sexes, but the dictatorial government where I lived did their best to prevent women from viewing themselves as valuable members of society. Add to the equation that as women, we have to work twice as hard as men to get to the point where we're considered successful, but that never stopped me. My father and mother were excellent role models who taught me that I could do anything if I just put my mind to it. It's important to me to raise my girls the same way as I was brought up when it comes to equality and to help them believe in themselves and their rights. I want them to know that if they find themselves in a bad situation that they can escape it, whether it be a job that makes them feel sad, an abusive spouse, or any predicament that makes them feel less of a woman or less of a human being. I want them to know that they can get up and go. This life is so short yet so valuable... and so are you. Choose happiness. Life can also be happier if you have the strength to demand what you deserve. *"The joy of life is in the journey."*

I believe that with hard work, there is no limitation on what you can do and achieve as long as you believe in yourself. I try to be an inspiration to those who think that it's "easier said than done". I am living proof that no matter what life throws at you and no matter how hard it was in your past, or how much you are struggling now in your present, it is you who dictates your future. If you fall down, get up again. *You are the one who is writing your book and only you can decide on how it ends*. Circumstances will exist and obstacles will appear in your way, but it is up to you to use them to your advantage and not allow them to destroy you.

We may not possess magic wands to fix all problems, but we can start by focusing on each other with love and care. Checking on your neighbor is just one example. If you see a single mother who is working hard, try to help and give her an hour break if you can. I am sure she needs it. Perform a kind gesture for someone. Kindness only multiplies and produces more kindness. Change begets change – and pretty soon, it has a positive domino effect.

***

Who could have ever predicted the life traveled by Hagir Elsheikh? Her journey began at an extremely young age and is far from over, but after reading where she's been, one would assume that she was telling the life story of a wonderful woman who is late in life, but no... she's only in her early forties.

While she guides, nurtures and sets an example for two teenage daughters to follow and shares her family with her new husband, while she grows and directs her own successful business and sets an example for all to follow especially in how to treat their employees, she still has taken time to follow her passions: total equality for all women, an end to female genital mutilation everywhere, an appreciation for the rights of all human beings and freedom for the oppressed and an end to starvation, an end to warfare and strife in her native Sudan – indeed, in the world, improved treatment of refugees everywhere, an end to human trafficking worldwide, and an end to spousal abuse and assistance and education for battered women everywhere. Her blogs, media appearances, writings, lectures and speeches bring those passions to the masses and spread her knowledge and experiences and allow her to indeed, achieve her goals – to make a difference in the world.

As the small child began her journey traveling through the sands of Tandalti in search of her destiny, the city's Elhakeem could never have imagined just how much of a difference his and his wife Buthina's thirteenth and youngest child would make in the world. The passion for humanity that he instilled in his daughter – his mission to not only bring medical services to his people but not to hesitate to be an activist against all inhumanity and an Islamic Government who only care about propagating themselves and don't care what happens to their people – would lead her to bring his message of dignity for all across the world. As he held his teen daughter's bloodied and bruised body that had been hung from a tree for hours and tortured beyond comprehension, he could never have dreamed what she would accomplish in so few years.

Through starvation and betrayal and the difficult road of a desperate refugee, his daughter, buoyed by the strength and support of family and friends, managed to escape a probable death warrant and began a new life in the United States only to become a victim again – a battered wife with two children, alone in a strange new land, betrayed by the one man she had trusted with her life. The strength and dignity that allowed her to survive numerous arrests and tortures was challenged as she became a battered spouse whose confidence and dignity were severely wounded by this abuse. But, through the strength and stubbornness she brought to Pennsylvania from Sudan, she rebuilt her confidence, stood tall with dignity and overcame each obstacle put in front of her. Through stubborn determination and a willingness to accept hard work as a way of life, she made a new life for herself and her daughters, built a successful business overcoming all the barriers women entrepreneurs face in the world, and now, she is bringing her message of love, equality and survival to anyone who will listen.

Little Hagir has indeed traveled many roads in her quest for life, and we believe that there are many more roads to travel – hopefully, without the pain and suffering of her past. As Elhakeem's small 4 year old beauty walked through the sands of Sudan beginning her quest, little did he know that her precocious mind would bring his message of freedom, equality and dignity throughout the world, that she would indeed, achieve her dream of *Climbing On The Clouds.*

About the Author

Hagir Elsheikh conducts her life like a well-choreographed dance, gracefully managing a myriad of projects with an air of calm confidence and conviviality. Hagir is an entrepreneur, an electrical engineer-turned registered nurse and juggles life as a mother with two daughters while running her company. She is best known for her Human Rights and Women's Rights activism and domestic violence advocacy. She struggled a lot from an early age but managed to keep a positive attitude and changed those negatives into success. Hagir experienced domestic violence after she fled political violence and torture in Sudan. She thought of herself as someone who could make a difference. After all, she was the spokesperson for the Sudanese Democratic Party during college. She fought a corrupt dictatorship in Sudan along with other activists; that put her life in danger, and she was forced to become a refugee and seek immigration to the US in search of a better life. She ended up facing violence in her own home.

Hagir uses her life story and her vision to influence, motivate and empower others. She became a motivational speaker. Her professional and personal visions merged together as one, once she found a career that she enjoyed. She became a Registered Nurse with a Bachelor of Science and Nursing Degree, and soon after, she started her own company where she is the owner and CEO of HSE Staffing Agency LLC – one of the leading health care staffing agencies in Central PA that pairs healthcare providers with skilled employees. She teaches at Harrisburg Area Community College (HACC) as a clinical instructor and advocates for victims of violence through Tomorrow's Smiles, LLC, her non-profit organization. When she is not running her company, Hagir volunteers at different organizations such as The Capital Coalition on Homelessness, the YWCA, the Meals on Wheels, Pennsylvania Alliance Against the

Trafficking of Humans and the Pennsylvania Coalition Against Domestic Violence. She was recently appointed to Harrisburg Area Community College Board of Trustees. She is also a member of the college's diversity committee. In 2019, she was named to the Board of Trustees of Church World Services (CWS). CWS is a worldwide refugee organization – an organization that played a significant role in bringing her to the United States. During her spare time, she creates podcasts on topics like human trafficking as a host of the TV talk show *The Hagir Show*, a co-host of *TSO Live* a radio live talk show.

Hagir's work hasn't gone unnoticed by the community at large. She was recognized in 2017 by the *Central Penn Business Journal* (CPBJ) as a "Women of Influence". According to CPBJ Publisher Shaun McCoach, nominations are independently scored based on their contributions to the community by judges who are selected from a list of past winners. "Based on her outstanding contributions to the community, it's no surprise that Hagir won," he said. It's tough not to marvel at Elsheikh. Many wonder how she manages to pack so much into her schedule without falling apart at the seams, but the fabric of her life seems to be woven of Kevlar, and she's overcome adversity time and again with grit, determination, hard work, and resilience. She was featured in many magazines, newspapers, Documentaries and TV shows in the US and internationally. Hagir was also the recipient of the health care hero award in 2017. Hagir's company was named Readers' Choice "Simply the Best" Staffing Agency in Central Pennsylvania for 2 years in a row: 2017 and 2018. Hagir was recently honored by the State of Pennsylvania with their Year of the Woman Recognition and in 2019 was inducted into the Grand Canyon University (GCU) Hall of Fame, representing their College of Nursing.

Hagir Elsheikh

Founder/CEO – HSE Staffing, LLC

Founder/CEO – Tomorrow's Smile, Inc

Host – *TSO Live* Talk Show

Host – *The Hagir Show*

Domestic Violence Counselor – Cumberland County, PA

Clinical Instructor/Faculty – HACC, Central Pennsylvania's Community College

Member, Board of Trustees – HACC, Central Pennsylvania's Community College

Works at – Capital Area Coalition on Homelessness

CPR/First Aid/AED Instructor – American Red Cross

Women's Rights Activist/Advocate – Tomorrow's Smile, Inc

Motivational Speaker – Tomorrow's Smile, Inc

Volunteer – Meals On Wheels American

Awards

GCU College of Nursing – Hall of Fame

State of Pennsylvania Year of the Woman Recognition

HSE named Reader's Choice Best Staffing Agency in Central Pennsylvania 2017 & 2018

Health Care Hero Award – 2017

Central Penn Business Journal (CPBJ) named her as – "Woman of Influence"

Acknowledgment

As with many things I have done in my life, this memoir and my journey would not have been possible without the help of many people around me who surrounded me with their love and support. Many thanks to everyone who helped me to make this dream a reality.

First and foremost, I am thankful to my parents, Buthina and Seed Ahmed who fostered within me a sense of responsibility and the belief that gender is no impediment to achieving one's goals. I would not be where I am today if it wasn't for their sacrifices, their way of modeling any behavior they wanted us to follow and their tireless effort to help others and fight for what they believed in.

That message follows me to this day, and I am raising my two daughters with those same standards. It is my wish that those who are struggling will read my story and perhaps be inspired, for there is nothing that can't be achieved if you possess grit, determination and a willingness to put in the hard work. To my beautiful young lady, Malaz, I have no doubt you will excel in anything and everything you set your mind to. You never cease to amaze me with your strength, ability and kindness. If there is a perfect child, that would be you. There is no limit to what you can do or be because you are that good. It is not a surprise to me that you got to where you're at. Every day is unique with you, and I can't imagine my life without your beautiful face, amazing personality and big, kind heart. You inspire me and make me proud every day with your exceptional strength, intelligence and ability to achieve anything you desire. I sometimes wonder how I got so lucky, but then, I remember that luck has nothing to do with it. Attention, time, dedication and nurturing is all our children need to blossom.

To Remaz, my sweet, kind, intelligent, artistic one, your big heart and caring personality are so refreshing. You surprise me every day with what you can do and accomplish. You are growing up to be this amazing young lady who cares about the world and everyone around her. It is no surprise to me that everyone who knows you loves you. You've impacted my life and many others in your eleven years in this world. I am sure you will continue to make a difference and put your marks anywhere you go. Keep aiming high and you will get further in life. I am thankful for your existence; without you, my world would have been so dull.

I am also thankful to my brothers: Rashid, Adel, Shukary, Sami, Haidar, Husham, Diaa and my sisters: Nagat and Nagla who helped me navigate this world. Thank you for always being there to guide me and love me regardless of the differences we sometimes had. I know I didn't make it easy for all of you to love me, but you always did and proved to me that a sibling's love is one of the purest unconditional loves that exists in this world.

Thanks to all my in-laws who came into our lives as strangers but soon, grew closer and made that invisible line between siblings and in-laws disappear.

Thanks to all my friends who kept me in line and gave me a reason to live and laugh again – especially: Waleed, Osman, and M. Idris who played a vital role in my life.

A very special thank you to: Tiffany, Heather, Mama Aisha, Angela, Wafa, Arvilla, Sara, and Fatima… who were the second mothers to my girls. I can't even imagine my life without you in it. You were my backbone and the shoulder I leaned on.

To my second family here in the US who became my shelter: Eltayeb, Raga, Alaa, AB, Israa, Moe and Faisal who showed me love and acceptance all the time.

Special thanks to my best friend, Eltayeb, who understands me without words and loves me unconditionally – even with thousands of miles between us, despite this distance our bond is still as strong as it was 20 some years ago. To my soul mate Khalid, the love of my life and the one person who made me believe in unconditional love, you will forever hold a special place in my heart. To Limya, who understands me so well even through my silence, your existence in this world made it much more tolerable.

To Magdi, you are the one who kept me sane with your wisdom and love. To Sara, Eldonglawi, Mussab, Amjad, Muhanad, Hind, and Huida, to my better half, Sahar Sona, Elfahal and Osama, I can't imagine what my life would've been like without you as a part of it. Muntasir and Kelly, Dr. Ali, Elshafi, Bakash, and Nahid, you all became my shelter and my safe haven.

Thank you to all my friends who haven't been mentioned here; all impacted my life some way or another during my long and eventful journey.

There are many other people who have contributed and helped me get through the difficult times, but to write about them all would be endless. Without them, my life would've been a complete struggle. I am thankful for my husband Hazim; your kind heart, warmth and bubbly personality made me fall in love with you. You make me laugh and show me every day that I made the right decision. Although we are at the very beginning of our journey, we know it will not be easy, but with determination and persistence, we will have many years to come – full of joy and laughter.

My thanks to my idol, Fatima Ibrahim and to Nelson Mandela who inspired me and to many other idols who helped to shape who I am today.

To Tom Peashey and Deb Sutton, I also believe that life sent me a treat for every obstacle I faced and circumstances have proven that to be the case. Through my adventures, I met many special people who came into my life during my dark times and made them brighter. You two came into my life to give me that push I needed to make this dream of telling my story to the world a reality. It is so funny that I waited all this time to finish this book and bring my adventures to life. Things were always in my way, preventing me from moving forward until I reached out for help, and Deb answered me all the way from her home near Calais, France. Without knowing anything about me, she offered me her knowledgeable and caring personality and, in the process, introduced me to an amazing person, her friend, Tom Peashey, who soon enough became my trusted friend, editor and collaborator. Without his additional storytelling, editing and passion about everything he has done, this book would still be on my desktop. So, thank you both for assisting in this amazing journey and for restoring my faith on people.

If I learned one thing from my ride in this world thus far, it is never to take anything for granted. Life has a way of humbling us, and anytime I felt I mastered this game of life, it proved me wrong. So, my advice is to live this life to the fullest and make your existence count. When you complete this journey, don't depart without leaving your marks. Make sure that your time here is worthy.

Tom Peashey - Author, Editor and Proof Reader

Tom Peashey is a retired international marketing and public relations person and expert in non-profit 501(c) organizations. Living on Lake Ontario near Rochester, N.Y., in his retirement, Tom has written several novels and ventured into editing/proofreading and has exceeded two hundred novels edited and published. For over sixty years, Tom was well known for his work in the Marching Music Activity as a performer, manager, adjudicator, arranger and director of marching bands, drum and bugle corps, winter guards and other similar groups – and in 2006, he was inducted into the World Drum Corps Hall of Fame and has received many other similar honors. Tom spends most of his time following his six grandchildren, all in the greater Rochester area. For further information about editing/proofreading projects, email: tompeashey@gmail.com or check out www.tompeashey.com.

APPENDIX

Meetings with U.S. Congress
Washington, DC – January 2019

As an effort to raise awareness and educate about the current situation in Sudan, The Sudanese Human Rights Network and Torture Abolition and Survivors Support Coalition (TASSC) facilitated a series of Meetings in Congress with congressional offices to educate policymakers about the protests in Sudan and the violence being carried out by the Sudanese security forces, attacking peaceful protestors who are calling for an end to the almost 30-year-old Bashir dictatorship regime. For that and many other violations by the Sudanese government, the activists explained they were deeply concerned by the ongoing widespread and gross human rights violations and abuses, and arbitrary detention by Sudanese authorities of peaceful demonstrators, civil society party members, oppositions' leaders, and activists.

The meetings were between twenty-seven minutes to forty minutes in length at time depending on the representative's availabilities. The two organizations composed a letter to Congress that was provided during these meetings with an attachment of an article about Sudan.

In those meetings, a group of Sudanese activists accompanied by a representative from TASSC, met with a Congress member's representative in a closed office meeting where every activist was allowed 5 minutes to talk about the situation. Prior to the meeting, the activists divided an area to be discussed in those five minutes to avoid repetition and used the available time wisely.

One activist discussed the fatalities and the brutal way that the government of Sudan is handling the peaceful and unarmed protesters. They gave them statistics on the death toll, the injuries

184

and the detainees with a complete description of how they were killed using snipers and a direct hit to the head, neck, and chest. We also talked about the use of live ammunition including the RIP Bullet, the use of rubber bullets and the injuries that resulted from it, the use of tear gas with the protesters as well as in people's houses and hospitals, the use of the police car to run over protesters and the attack to peoples' houses and places of work.

*The government is targeting professionals, killing doctors for simply helping the injured protesters and lawyers for defending the victims.

*Since 1989 the government has caused great stress to the country, destroyed the economy and sold major projects in Sudan.

*The situation in Sudan deteriorated and continued to deteriorate which caused the people of Sudan to seek refuge on the street as an alternative to dying at home from hunger.

*Many activists protested against this government from 1989 to present, and many were killed, injured and detained. Many people were forced to leave the country and seek a refugee status somewhere else. Many stayed and continue fighting under those circumstances.

*One of the major revolutions started in September 2013 as a peaceful protest where people marched calling for peace, freedom, and justice. The government responded by killing over 200 young protesters point blank.

*Since December 2018 up to today, the street is filled with the largest protests ever demanding the end of President Bashir's rule.

*The death toll from the peaceful protest in Sudan is over fifty-one, over three thousand detainees one hundred fifty-seven women arrested and many uncounted for.

Another activist discussed the long history of Al-Bashir and its regime and reminded the congress their involvement in Darfur Genocide, the ethnic cleansing and crimes in the Nubian mountains, South Kordofan and South Sudan as well as the death toll in 2013 revolution. They also discussed the effect of this government on that region and the US and why it is imperative to act now and help the revolution by answering why the US should care.

The activist pointed out that:

*The Government of Sudan is one of the biggest threats to peace and stability in the region. They Still Provide opportunities for spreading extremist Islamic ideologies to African students and prepare them through the International University of Africa, a public University that is a member of the Federation of the Universities of the Islamic World and based in Khartoum, Sudan.

*The government of Sudan is China's Original Foothold in Africa. In June 1997, the Greater Nile Petroleum Operating Company was established with the China National Petroleum Corporation (CNPC) taking forty percent ownership and Malaysia's Petronas taking thirty percent. India's ONGC Videsh acquired twenty-five percent when a forerunner of Canada's Talisman Energy had to leave due to sanctions. China has invested in other aspects of the industry until it now controls as much as seventy-five percent of the Sudanese oil industry. Chinese investments in Africa comes at the expense of Human Rights in Africa.

*The Government of Sudan's relationship with Russia continued for decades; there are economic, political and military relations between the two countries. In 2008, rebels from Darfur killed a Russian mercenary pilot by shooting his plane down. Al-Bashir asked Putin for 'protection' from the US during their meeting in the Black Sea resort of Sochi, Russia, Nov. 23, 2017. Russia investments in Sudan and Africa come at the expense of Human Rights in Africa.

*Al-Bashir of Sudan is one of the World's Most Ruthless Dictators. There is an international warrant for his arrest on charges of war crimes and genocide. His stay in power is a real threat to the region and the world's peace and stability. He does not seem to care if his country disintegrated or lives in chaos in exchange for his personal safety!

They also reminded the Congress that many credible human rights reports, including that of the U.S. Department of State, documented that government forces have attacked civilians in west and south regions of Sudan, specifically in Darfur, Southern Kordofan and the Blue Nile on several occasions during the past year.

Another activist discussed what they want the Congress to do in a letter and their speech. The activist urges the Congress to:

*Call on the Sudanese government to immediately stop its atrocities and violent crackdown on peaceful protesters, end the unjustifiable arrest of peaceful demonstrators and release all political detainees.

*To tell Omar Al-Bashir to listen to the demands of the Sudanese people and step aside so an interim transitional government can assume power and plan for fair elections.

*Call for an international and independent investigation on the killing and torture of peaceful protesters in Sudan.

*Call for an investigation regarding Mohammed Al Atta's involvement with the NISS and Darfur Genocide and immediately expel and remove M. Al Atta from his diplomatic duty and the US.

*Request a press release and tweets to be sent from Congress regarding the situation in Sudan and demanding action.

After the activists took their turn speaking, the representative asked questions and explained to the activists what they can and can't do. Many representatives in those meetings were also part of the African subcommittee on Foreign Affairs including the committee chair, Karen Bass.

They informed the activists that the Congress members are working on a resolution for Sudan and they talked about how we can help to speed this process by writing to the officials.

The activists also asked for an emergency hearing which the representatives stated they will pass this on to their meeting next week, but they can't promise the emergency hearing will be granted.

The representative also mentioned that since the government was in a shut down for a while, there are many issues on the table that might cause a delay, but they are aware of the urgency of the situation.

Follow up emails will be sent and Thursday 1/31 meetings were with the following congress members' offices:
Congress Donald McEachin Democrat from Virginia
Congress Albio sires Democrat from New Jersey
Congress Karen Bass Democrat from California
Congress Chrissy Houlahan Democrat from Pennsylvania.

Friday 2/1/19 meetings had two delegations (two groups of Sudanese activists and TASSC representatives)

The first delegation met with the following congress members' offices:

Congress James Raskin Democrat from Maryland

Congress Frank Pallone Democrat from New Jersy.

Congress John Curtis Rebuplican from Utah.

Congress Ilhan Omar Democrat Minnesota.

The second delegation met with the following congress members' offices:

Congress Ami Bera- Democrat from California

Congress John Sarbanes- Democrat Maryland

Congress Ken Buck- Republican from Colorado

A BRIEF HISTORY OF
THE PRIOR REVOLUTIONS IN SUDAN

1956: Sudan gains independence.

1958: A military coup takes place in Sudan. The civilian government is removed.

1962: The civil war breaks out in the southern (mainly Christian/African) parts of Sudan.

October 1964: People of Sudan rebel. The military junta falls after a communist general strike. A national government is formed.

May 1969: New military coup placing Jaafar Numeiri takes power.

1971: Leaders of the communist party are executed for attempting a coup against Numeiri.

1972: A peace agreement is signed in Addis Ababa. The southern Sudan achieves partial self-governance.

1978: Large findings of oil are made in Bentiu, southern Sudan. The oil becomes an important factor in the strife between North and South.

1983: Numieri introduces the Islamic Sharia law to Sudan leading to a new breakout of the civil war in the Christian south. In the south, the forces are led by the Sudan People's Liberation Movement (SPLM) under command by John Garang.

1985: President Numieri is removed from power in a military coup.

1986: A civilian government is made in an effort to restore peace after general elections.

1989: Al-Bashir and his Islamic Front (NIC) take power in a military coup.

1995: The Sudanese government is accused of being part of an attempt on the life of Egyptian Prime Minister Mubarak. UN decides on sanctions against Sudan.

US ATTACK ON SUDAN

1998: USA launches a missile attack on a chemical plant in Khartoum assumed to develop chemical weapons possibly in cooperation with the Al Qaeda terror network. Civilians are killed in the attack. The Sudanese government denies any link to terror and chemical weapons.

1998: A new constitution in Sudan.

1999: The president dissolves the national assembly and declares state of emergency.

1999: Sudan starts an export of oil assisted by China, Canada, Sweden and other countries.

2001: An internal struggle in the government, leads to the arrest of an ideological leader who were making peace attempts with the Sudan People's Liberation Army (SPLA)

March 2001: Hunger and famine in Sudan affects 3 million people.

May 2001: A Danish pilot flying for the International Red Cross is attacked and killed when delivering aid in southern Sudan. All flights in the area are temporarily stopped.

June 2001: Peace negotiations break down in Nairobi, Kenya.

August 2001: The Nile river floods leaving thousands homeless in Sudan.

September 2001: the UN lifts sanctions against Sudan to support ongoing peace negotiations.

October 2001: Following the New York terror attacks, USA puts new sanctions on Sudan due to accusations of Sudan's involvement with international terrorism.

During 2001: More than 14,550 slaves are freed after pressure from human rights groups.

NEW HOPE FOR PEACE?

January 2002: A ceasefire between government forces and the SPLM are finally agreed upon.

July 20th 2002: the government and SPLA signs a protocol to end the civil war.

July 27th 2002: President Al-Bashir meets for the first time with SPLA leader John Garang. Ugandan president Yoweri Museveni has arranged the meeting. The war in Sudan is also having huge impact on the northern Uganda.

July 31st 2002: Government attacks SPLA again.

October 2002: The ceasefire is confirmed again, but remains very uncertain. Peace negotiations still continue during the next year.

February 2003: The two rebel groups representing the African population in Darfur start a rebellion against the government as protest against neglect and suppression.

December 2003: Progress is made in the peace negotiations. The negotiations are mainly focused on sharing the important oil-resources.

ETHNIC KILLINGS IN DARFUR

January 2004: Government army strikes down an uprising in Darfur region in the Western Sudan. More than 100,000 people seek refuge in Chad.

March 2004: UN officers report that systematic killings of villagers are taking place in Darfur. UN names Darfur as the worst humanitarian problem currently, but nothing happens. UN fails to take action as Western countries and media have close to no focus on the problems in Sudan. But even the African leaders refuse to take action on the problem.

May 26th 2004: A historic peace agreement is signed, but the situation in Darfur remains unchanged and extremely critical.

January 9th 2005: In Nairobi, the government and rebels sign the last parts of the peace treaty for Southern Sudan. All fighting in Africa's longest civil war is expected to end in January 2005, but the peace agreement still doesn't cover the Darfur region. More than 1.5 million people lost their homes since the conflict in Darfur broke out early 2003.

March 15th 2005: United Nations Security Council agrees to send 10,000 peacekeeping soldiers to Southern Sudan. Again, the decision does not cover the Darfur region.

2007: Violence and killings continues in the Darfur region. The conflict is in reality a genocide and is still considered the worst humanitarian disaster in the world. But not much is done about it. China has large oil interests in Africa and Sudan in particular. UN sanctions and security forces are needed, but China blocks any real decisions in the UN security council. The rest of the world is not applying the necessary political pressure on the governments in Sudan and China.

SUDAN – A BRIEF TIMELINE

1956 Sudan becomes independent.

1958 General Ibrahim Abboud leads a military coup against the civilian government elected earlier in the year

1962 Civil war begins in the south, led by the Anya Nya movement.

1964 The "October Revolution" overthrows Abboud and an Islamist-led government is established

1969 Jaafar Numeiri leads the military coup.

1971 Sudanese Communist Party leaders executed after a short-lived coup against Mr. Numeiri.

1972 Under the Addis Ababa peace agreement between the government and the Anya Nya, the south becomes a self-governing region.

1978 Oil discovered in Bentiu in southern Sudan.

1983 Civil war breaks out again in the south involving government forces and the Sudan People's Liberation Movement (SPLM), led by John Garang.

1983 President Numeiri declares the introduction of Sharia Islamic law.

1985 After widespread popular unrest, Mr. Numeiri is deposed by a Transitional Military Council.

1986 Coalition government formed after elections, with Sadiq al-Mahdi as prime minister.

1989 National Salvation Revolution takes over in a military coup.

1993 General Omar Al-Bashir became the President.

1999 President Bashir dissolves the National Assembly and declares a state of emergency following a power struggle with parliamentary speaker, Hassan al-Turabi.

1999 Sudan begins to export oil.

2004 January - Army moves to quell rebel uprising in the western region of Darfur; hundreds of thousands of refugees flee to neighboring Chad. Pro-government Arab Janjaweed militias carry out systematic killings of non-Arab villagers in Darfur.

194

2004 March - Army officers and opposition politicians, including Islamist leader Hassan al-Turabi, are detained over an alleged coup plot.

2004 September - US Secretary of State Colin Powell describes Darfur killings as genocide.

2005 January - Government and southern rebels sign a peace deal.

2005 March - UN Security Council authorizes sanctions against those who violate ceasefire in Darfur. Council also votes to refer those accused of war crimes in Darfur to International Criminal Court.

2005 June - Government and exiled opposition grouping - National Democratic Alliance (NDA) - sign reconciliation deal allowing NDA into power-sharing administration.

2005 July - Former southern rebel leader John Garang is sworn in as first vice-president, new constitution gives a large degree of autonomy to the south.

2005 August - John Garang killed in plane crash, succeeded by Salva Kiir.

2006 May - Khartoum government and the main rebel faction in Darfur, the Sudan Liberation Movement, sign a peace accord. Two smaller rebel groups reject the deal. Fighting continues.

2007 July - UN Security Council approves a resolution authorizing a 26,000-strong force for Darfur. Sudan says it will co-operate with the United Nations-African Union Mission in Darfur (Unamid).

2008 May - Tension increases between Sudan and Chad after Darfur rebel group mounts a raid on Omdurman, Khartoum's twin city across the Nile. Sudan accuses Chad of involvement and breaks off diplomatic relations. Intense fighting breaks out between northern and southern forces in the disputed oil-rich town of Abyei. President Bashir and southern leader Salva Kiir agree to seek international arbitration to resolve a dispute over Abyei.

2009 March - The International Criminal Court in The Hague issues an arrest warrant for President Bashir on charges of war crimes and crimes against humanity in Darfur.

2009 July - North and south Sudan say they accept a ruling by the arbitration court in The Hague shrinking disputed Abyei region and placing the major Heglig oil field in the north.

2009 December - Leaders of North and South reach a deal on terms of a referendum on independence due in South by 2011.

2010 Feb-March - The Justice and Equality Movement (Jem) main Darfur rebel movement signs a peace accord with the government, prompting President Bashir to declare the Darfur war over. But failure to agree on specifics and continuing clashes with smaller rebel groups endanger the deal.

2010 July - International Criminal Court issues a second arrest warrant for President al-Bashir - this time on charges of genocide.

2010 August - Mr. Bashir tests ICC arrest warrant by visiting Kenya, an ICC signatory. The Kenyan government refuses to enforce the warrant. He later ignores South African court order not to leave the country in 2015.

2011 July - South Sudan gains independence after January popular vote, but some border areas remain in dispute.

2011 December - Government forces kill key Darfur rebel leader Khalil Ibrahim.

2012 May - Sudan pledges to pull its troops out of the border region of Abyei, which is also claimed by South Sudan, as bilateral peace talks resume.

2012 June - Protests in Khartoum against austerity measures after government cuts fuel and other subsidies in response to the drop in oil revenue after the independence of South Sudan.

2013 March - Sudan and South Sudan agree to resume pumping oil, ending a shutdown caused by a dispute over fees more than a year earlier, and to withdraw troops from their borders to create a demilitarized zone.

2013 September - Another wave of demonstrations over subsidies cuts. Scores of people die in clashes.

2013 October - Dissident members of ruling National Congress Party threaten split to reach out to secularists and leftists.

2013 December - President Bashir drops long-time ally and first vice president Ali Osman Taha from the cabinet in a major shake-up.

2014 December - The chief prosecutor of the International Criminal Court halts investigations into war crimes in Darfur for lack of support from the UN Security Council.

2016 November-December - Street and stay-at-home protests at IMF-prompted price hikes for basic goods. Government disperses protests, arrests opposition politicians, bans media coverage.

2017 October - the US announces the partial lifting of sanctions.

2018 January - Protests against bread price rises after the government removed subsidies.

2019 January - Large protests demand the end of President Bashir's rule after weeks of demonstrations against rises in the cost of living, in which up to 40 people died.

Made in the USA
Middletown, DE
13 December 2019